# WILDFLOWERS NEVER DIE

## The CIA and Memories of the Cold War

D1522340

RANDALL HOWLETT
DEB TURNBULL DEVRIES

"Remember your humanity and forget all the rest"

- Bertrand Russell

# Table of Contents

# Foreword

Randall Howlett and Deb Turnbull Devries present what Howlett describes as the "evils of communism, not so much about the ideology, but rather its authoritarian leaders having near absolute power." Mao is their big, bulbous target but they also pound on Stalin, Kruschev and others. The authors perceive the CIA as an unleashed "evil" that often must use its evil to fight against greater evil.

The authors also bring to life some of the CIA's more gruesome monsters stalking Asia, reeking of bloody coups and industrial-level slaughter in U.S. warfare. "The Frankenstein makers are the totalitarian societies and the CIA are townspeople with their axes and pitchforks," Howlett says "and unarmed villagers are countries and people used by the CIA as their surrogates in this epic and continuing battle."

> Richard S. Ehrlich is a Bangkok-based, American foreign correspondent reporting from Asia since 1978.

# Introduction

The authors came up with the idea of writing this book about a year ago, as a result of a social media discussion concerning Camp Hale in Colorado. Back in 1971, we had both graduated from a small mountain high school not more than ten miles from where the camp was located, a site for training the 10th Mountain Division in World War II. What we didn't know until much later, however, was that the CIA had also been training Tibetan freedom fighters there as well during the late fifties and early sixties. So, we initially decided to write about that period but as the narrative developed and facing a shortage of first-hand accounts, we chose to expand the subject to include the first thirty years of the Cold War.

While the secret training of Tibetans taking place under our noses was intriguing, it was the events spanning over three decades that influenced and shaped our lives in a multitude of ways. Such as, my father operating as a double agent for fourteen years while working for NATO, myself living in Spain where one of the world's worst nuclear bomb accidents took place, and Deb's husband having worked in the Titan missile silos in Kansas, then later drafted into the trauma that was the Vietnam War. And we certainly are not alone. The first thirty years of the Cold War and resulting conflicts affected a whole generation of people, friend and foe alike. This book is really for and about all of us.

# PART ONE (1947-1954)

# Blood and Hunger

The Soviet Union had declared war on Japan in August 1945, liberating both Manchuria and northern Korea from the Japanese Army. Mao knew that the civil war against Chiang Kai-shek's Nationalist Party would quickly resume now that their fight with the Japanese was out of the way. He'd been thinking for some time about how to position his Communist troops for the next round of hostilities and sending more men into Manchuria was a key element of that plan. Communist strategy had now largely transitioned from guerrilla raiding into full-scale mobile warfare. The man who had fought by Mao's side since the 1920s, General Lin Biao, was chosen to lead that effort in Manchuria. [8]

Lin Biao's tactics actually differed from Mao's. They were more complex than the typical "human wave" stereotype most would associate with the Chinese's Army. Lin was also willing to accept heavy casualties provided, however, such losses were the price to be paid for achieving a necessary objective. He was concerned with minimizing needless casualties, so he suggested to higher command the idea of first sealing off complete access to the city of Changchun. [8]

By June 1948, Mao had agreed to Lin Bao's proposal to deal with Changchun first by putting it under a multi-month-long siege, followed up by a military attack. Specifically...

> "The goals of the siege were to cut off the enemy's supplies of grain and fuel, to prohibit anyone from entering or leaving the city, to close off all the airports both inside and outside city limits, disrupt the airdrop of supplies, annihilate any enemy units that might try to

> break out of the siege, and prepare eventually to attack and capture Changchun.
>
> "On the ground, Communist forces constructed multiple barrier layers. First, was a ring of trenches, barbed wire, and fortified defense works, then a second line of defensive works." [8, 11]

Young Homare Endo's father was a Japanese technician working in Changchun when the Nationalist army took over the city in May 1946, following Japanese surrender. Being a person possessing critically needed skills, they wouldn't allow him to be repatriated like most other Japanese later that year. The family was still stuck there when Mao's Communist forces sealed off and laid siege to Changchun two years later. While she was only in the second grade at the time, Homare vividly recalls those events and the devastating impact of starvation.... [11]

> "People were eating horses, dogs, cats, rats and birds.... anything that could be killed and eaten. The dogs had taken to eating the bodies of children who had just died. Corpses could be seen almost everywhere. Children who had lost their parents were often pushed out into the street, calling for their mother and father. They were easy targets for starving dogs, which had reverted to their feral status and acquired a taste for human flesh." [11]

Homare goes on further to say...

> "By this time, everyone in my family were all horribly emaciated and deathly pale, our skin covered with dark wrinkles as if we had suddenly become very old. Our ribs stood out starkly like those of a skeleton in the desert, leaving our bloated stomachs bulging out below.

"Our arms and legs had become bony sticks that made
a hard clacking sound when they bumped up against
one another. There seemed to be nothing separating
the skin and the bones. The skin became loose and
slack, and if you pulled it with your fingers, it just hung
there where you had let it go." [11]

Homare Endo lost several siblings to starvation before the family managed to
escape the city through a lone exit corridor that had become available. The
starvation of Changchun's civilian population was something the Communist
Army fully expected, if not intended. It had become an integral part of their war
strategy. In order to maximize the political impact of civilian suffering, one
Communist leader pointed out that,

"We should place the blame for the ordinary people's
starvation and poverty squarely on the shoulders of the
enemy (Kuomintang) army and the enemy government,
then exaggerate the contradiction between them and
the masses." [11]

The deaths of an estimated 150,000 civilians during the siege of Changchun
contrasted with the Communist Party's projected image as a force for liberation
of common people from the evils of Chiang Kai-shek's regime. A Peoples
Liberation Army colonel later wrote that the casualties as compared with
Hiroshima were about the same. Hiroshima took nine seconds while the agony
of Changchun dragged on for five months. His 1989 book, not surprisingly,
would later be banned in China. [8]

The Chinese Army ended up prevailing in Changchun after the Nationalist's
much vaunted First Army was forced to surrender. Many of Chiang Kai-shek's
soldiers simply ended up changing sides near the end of the battle. After
achieving decisive victories in the Liaoshen, Huaihai and Pingjin campaigns, the
Communist Army ended up eliminating 144 regular and 29 irregular Nationalist
divisions, including taking their tanks, artillery and combined arms, thus

significantly reducing Nationalist military might. Much of that equipment had been supplied to Chiang's army, courtesy of the United States. [8]

The Kuomintang actually made a final attempt to use Tibetan Khampa troops against the Communists in southwest China. The plan was for three Khampa divisions, assisted by the Panchen Lama, to oppose the Communists. Kuomintang intelligence reported that some Tibetan chiefs controlled up to 80,000 troops in Sichuan, Qinghai and Tibet but the plan was never put into motion. [8]

Mao would press on to capture Nanjing, the Nationalist capital, forcing Chiang's forces to escape to several successive cities before finally retreating to Taiwan on December 7, 1949. He had proclaimed the founding of the People's Republic of China two months earlier, whereas Chiang Kai-shek would continue to assert his government, now in Taiwan, continued to be the legitimate authority of mainland China. [8, 11]

# A Boy of Stone

The young boy was scolded by his father in front of family guests, which embarrassed and enraged him, so he called his father several names before storming out of the house. The angry father gave chase, demanding that the boy return. The boy ignored his father and upon reaching the edge of a nearby lake, he threatened to jump in. The father ended up backing down. Retelling this story in later years, the young man explained, "Old men don't want to lose their sons, that is their weakness and I attacked at the weak point." The boy's childhood nickname would become Shi San Ya-zi, which meant, "A Boy of Stone." Mao Tse-Tung would continue using the same term, which he was immensely proud of... well into early adulthood. [1]

Mao was born and reared from peasant stock in the Shaoshan Valley of Hunan Province. In the year 1893, the valley was a place of ancient beauty, with undulating green hills shrouded in mist, traversed by calming streams and pockmarked with ancient temples. It was in this deep heartland of China where Buddhism had first arrived during the Tang Dynasty. This is, however, where any similarity between Mao Tse-Tung and ancient culture, religion, and concern for the welfare of Chinese peasants ends. [1]

Mao Tse-Tung was also never really an avid Communist. His lack of heartfelt commitment would result in an unusual relationship between him and the Chinese Communist party, even after he became its Chairman. He wasn't friends with any political colleagues and unlike other totalitarian leaders like Hitler, Mussolini or Stalin, he wasn't a great orator or inspiring speaker. Mao's method was to simply find people who were loyal and willing to follow his dictates.

## Part One (1947-1954)

Others were usually eliminated in some manner or another. Not unlike chess pieces, they were expendable pawns, no longer needed in his quest to build and consolidate power. [1]

Mao's personality embodied two primary characteristics. First of all, he didn't agree that to be a moral person, one's actions had to benefit others. He believed he had no responsibility to others nor toward future generations and could care less about his legacy or what he left behind. The other element or characteristic was the pleasure he felt with the process of destruction and upheaval, saying...

> "When great heroes give full play to their impulses,
> they are magnificently powerful, stormy and invincible."
> [1]

These personality traits firmly took hold by the time he was only twenty-four years old. Later, on a month-long trip through Hunan Province in 1927, after witnessing the brutal actions of peasant association bosses, his attitude towards using violence was bolstered. He came to recognize its effectiveness, particularly when instilling fear in unexpected and arbitrary ways. Fear could bend colleagues as well as the masses to his will, that inspiring oratory alone could not. Everyone could be held in check. [1]

# National Security Act

The Central Intelligence Agency's birth was a somewhat difficult one, given its inherent need for secrecy and using methods likely to conflict with core tenets of a democracy. Concepts that included transparency, due process and accountability would be sorely challenged. Early on, the CIA would also be confronted with matters of moral ambiguity in a nation which prides itself as a beacon of human rights. From its very inception, the agency was confronted with naysayers and critics...

> "I had the gravest forebodings about this organization and warned the President that neither he, the National Security Council, nor anyone else would be in a position to know what it was doing or to control it", warned Dean Acheson, future Secretary of State. [2]

It faced relentless attacks from the Defense Department as well as the State Department over where the agency properly belonged, assuming even if it did belong. Its creation was even feared by some as becoming an American version of the Gestapo, the heinous scourge of fascism that had just been defeated. It needed a strong proponent—someone with the ardent conviction of the need for an intelligence service, who also had the credentials and experience of having served in a clandestine organization. That person would be Allen W. Dulles, who served with the CIA's predecessor Office of Strategic Services (OSS) during World War II. Dulles, interestingly, just happened to be born the same year as Mao in 1893. He even had a few of the same character traits of being duplicitous, an adulterer and not above misleading those believed to be obstructing his ambitions. Fortunately, however, he was tempered by religious and egalitarian convictions... and he was on our side. [2, 42]

> "Americans already had the raw material for building the greatest intelligence service in the world," Dulles said. He described "a CIA that would be directed by a relatively small but elite corps of men with a passion for anonymity." Its director would require "judicial temperament in high degree, with long experience and profound knowledge." [2]

And so, the National Security Act of 1947 was born out of remnants of World War II's Office of Strategic Services (OSS) and need to address a world now menaced by communist aggression. A threat that the world would face disaster unless the United States fought the scourge, head on. What began as the Truman Doctrine became an act of Congress establishing in July 1947, the office of Secretary of Defense, a separate Air Force, the National Security Council and several months later, the Central Intelligence Agency. [42, 50]

Aside from attacks by the Departments of State and Defense largely over jurisdictional and reporting issues, the Act authorizing the CIA dealt with functions related to intelligence gathering. Use of covert measures were not addressed yet to counter communist developments in Italy, Czechoslovakia, Berlin and Greece which also required funding. Thus began the Marshall Plan in 1948 which appropriated over $13.7 billion during a five-year period to reconstruct war-torn Europe. In addition to the plan's founders, Allen Dulles would be named as its consultant. The government's objective was to shape Europe into a likeness of the United States, countering the efforts of Joseph Stalin. That meant five percent of the allocated funds, or $685 million would be available for use by the CIA as a secret, untraceable source to pay for covert activities. The use of funding from alternative sources would become a more common practice for the agency in the years to come. [2, 42, 50]

Now with a seemingly inexhaustible bankroll, the CIA needed better structuring to more easily plan and carry out their cloaked operations. That fell to the Office of Policy Coordination (OPC) which was placed within the CIA but would report to the secretaries of state and defense instead. It was soon recognized that the OPC really needed only a single person in charge and that job fell to Frank Wisner. Before long, his organization soon grew bigger than the rest of the CIA combined. Covert operations became the agency's dominant force, with the most people, the most money, and also the most power. It grew rapidly during the Korean War and would eventually merge in August 1952 with the Office of Special Operations, becoming the Directorate of Plans. Allen Dulles would take charge as the Assistant Director under Walter Bedell Smith, and in 1953, he became the Director of the CIA. [42, 50]

Allen Dulles was Eisenhower's man at the CIA when he was elected President. The agency was now streamlined for greater efficiency and provided the President more viable options to counter communist expansion and aggression. Taking the Truman Doctrine yet another step would be Eisenhower's "New Look" national security policy. It focused on balancing the need for national security with the commensurate financial costs to the nation. It emphasized strategic nuclear weapons, thereby lowering the exorbitant cost needed to maintain high troop levels of conventional forces. Employing the use of tactical nuclear weapons was also a factor that was seriously considered once those weapons went into production during the mid-1950s. [4]

> "As to tactical nuclear weapons on strictly military targets and for strictly military purposes, I can see no reason why they shouldn't be used just exactly as you would use a bullet or anything else," President Eisenhower said. [2]

The New Look Policy also embodied an increased reliance on the use of covert operations and espionage. Their benefits were exhibited during the early days of the Cold War and was considered relatively inexpensive in relation to other options. Appointed Secretary of State around the time his younger brother Allen came onboard, John Foster Dulles, provided Eisenhower the heft in implementing his New Look Policy. Working separately or in tandem, the Dulles brothers would become Eisenhower's most valued advisors on national security during the 1950s. [4, 42]

The President also had the Joint Chiefs of Staff (JCS) to rely on as advisors as did the Secretary of Defense. Members in 1950 included the Army, Navy and Air Force with the Chairman being General Omar Bradley, Eisenhower's trusted deputy during World War II. Fortunately, they worked well together because by 1949, the Soviets now had their own atomic bomb and relentlessly expanded their aggression throughout Eastern Europe to include Iran and Turkey. China was also passing within their orbit as later would Southeast Asia. No sooner than the Soviets test their first atomic bomb in Kazakhstan than talk began in the US of developing a thermonuclear one based on fusion of hydrogen isotopes. In other words, the Superbomb. According to a CIA study then, the Soviet Union would be able to produce two hundred atomic bombs by 1954, leading the US to focus on the nuclear-capable Soviets rather than China. The Russians were devoting twice the percentage the US was of their national budget for military purposes. [2, 42, 50]

With a renewed sense of urgency, the JCS developed the Joint Outline Emergency War Plan (JOEWP), codenamed OFFTACKLE, which outlined how World War III would likely unfold and the US strategic response that needed to be taken. While the brainstorming occurred on a global-wide basis, a more conventional but major conflict was about to break out on the Korean Peninsula... right when the military was downsizing and hoping to enjoy a hard-fought peace dividend from World War II. Remembering Hiroshima, the thought of using nuclear weapons in the context of a conventional war would again enter into discussions by the JCS and National Security Council. [4, 42, 50]

# The Candy Bombers

Rummaging through the big canvas mail bag, Lieutenant Halvorsen spotted a letter which appeared to be addressed to him. Carefully opening the envelope, a smile appeared across his weary face. He'd been flying airlifts continuously for weeks and was dog-tired. Looking forward to a few hours of shut-eye before tomorrow's sorties, the words from seven-year-old Mercedes made his day...

> "Dear Chocolate Pilot,
>
> We live near the airfield at Tempelhof, and our chickens think your airplanes are chicken hawks so they become frightened when you fly over to land. They run into the shelter with no more eggs from them. It is a big problem for us. We need the eggs. But when you fly over the garden and see the white chickens, please drop some candy there and all will be ok. I don't care if you scare them.
>
> Your little friend,
> Mercedes" [99]

Lieutenant Gail Halvorsen was part of a massive joint allied effort to fly-in food and supplies into West Berlin. It all started in late June 1948 and my father was a part of a monumental effort to keep over two million people alive and later also warm for the winter. For dad, then twenty-two years old, the Berlin Airlift was a proud start to his military career, with him being a contributing member of the occupation forces. In fact, the airlift would be considered by many authors and historians alike, to be America's finest moment. People were saved and the

## Part One (1947-1954)

US stood up to the tyranny of Stalin, whom we believed to be a wartime ally. [98]

Joseph Stalin had designs of his own, however; they were designs he'd developed at the Potsdam Conference in July 1945 but more likely years before. At the conference in Potsdam, Germany, the three powers of Great Britain, the US and Soviet Union met to decide on the partitioning of Germany into occupation zones. One region would be allocated to the French as well. The participants wanted to avoid earlier mistakes that occurred during the Paris Peace Conference of 1919. At Potsdam, Truman also made it known to Stalin that a successful atomic bomb test had just taken place days before near Alamogordo, New Mexico. Of course, Stalin already was well aware, since his spies had infiltrated the Manhattan Project, pilfering the means for the Soviets to build their own bomb. Many things had changed since the prior conference back in February in Yalta. Since that time, the Red Army would go on to take over Poland, Czechoslovakia, Hungary, Bulgaria and Romania.

The Soviet Union agreed at Potsdam to finally enter the war against the Japanese now that Europe was wrapped up. His soldiers in Manchuria would be noteworthy for their lack of military discipline and inhumanity. They attacked and raped Japanese civilians. In one notable instance, when Japanese women and children escaped to a Tibetan Buddhist temple, the refugees were shot, run over by tanks and trucks and bayoneted while holding a white surrender flag. At the end of two hours, over a thousand civilians lay dead. Many of the Soviet soldiers committing the atrocities had been transferred from the European front where mass rape by Soviet soldiers first began during the Battle of Romania and the Budapest Offensive. Stalin's response to reports of brutality was, "We lecture our soldiers too much, let them have their fun." The rapes intensified in the German occupied areas where up to two million women were known to have been raped, many publicly and in front of husbands or family. [98]

The western allies had given the Soviets a two-month leeway before their own forces entered Berlin. Many cities were devastated by the Russian and allied soldiers but also by British and American bombing. Eighty percent of historic buildings in Germany's main cities were leveled. Some cities, however, largely escaped destruction, like Wiesbaden, located just 25 miles west of Frankfurt. It was a spa city close to the Rhine River and would become Headquarters for US Air Forces in Europe where my father was stationed during the airlift.

Germans, and Berliners in particular, had every cause to be more angry at Americans and the British. While the Soviets bombed in 1941 and then again in 1945, it was the US, UK and—on occasion—the French who did the strategic or carpet bombing. Most of Berlin was left in rubbles with 600,000 apartments destroyed and only 2.8 million of the original 4.3 million inhabitants remaining in the city. Forty percent of the city's residents had fled, while thousands would be killed and 450,000 left homeless. Cities like Hamburg, Cologne, Munich, Frankfurt and of course Berlin would generate huge piles of rubble which would sometimes be given names. Berlin's piles would take years to remove or recycle but one was left standing and it was eventually covered with soil and natural growth. Its biggest pile, at a height reaching 394 feet, was called Teufelsberg, or Devil's Mountain. [98]

In 1946, an election with almost 93 percent voter turnout was held in Berlin with the non-communists garnering most of the vote. It was a clear repudiation of the party favored by the Soviet Union. The German people, wanting to chart their own direction, had enough of Russians and communist ways. However, voter preference be damned, Stalin was not about to let Berlin escape from the Soviet orbit. His grand vision was to get the British to first capitulate, believing the Americans would follow a year or two later. He believed that if Berlin succumbed to communism, so would Germany and as Germany goes so goes Europe. It was the firmly held belief of Stalin and his Foreign Minister, Vyacheslav Molotov at the time that Berlin was about to become one of the first Cold War hotspots. [98]

In 1947, Lieutenant Halvorsen was flying foreign transports out of Brookley Air Force Base in Mobile, Alabama. The military air transport operations primarily used C-54 and C-74 aircraft; Halvorsen qualified with the C-54 while in Brazil. He had been in the country after the war, ferrying equipment and searching for downed aircraft in the vast Amazon. Halvorsen was just about to leave the service when, one day in July 1948, an opportunity to continue flying presented itself. They were looking for pilots for Operation Vittles, which meant flying in food and fuel to the citizens of war-torn Berlin, Germany. After some introspection, Halvorsen decided to volunteer... [99]

> "I reflected on my own feelings about the German people. There was much in the media about the hardness of the Germans, the atrocities, and the claims of superiority. Some Americans had offered a defense by blaming the reported behavior on Hitler and his policies and not on the nature of people." [99]

> "Some of the airlift pilots had bombed Germany and Berlin during the war and we all felt that the Germans were the enemy. Our folks at home who were not involved as soldiers or pilots, also had negative feelings toward the Germans too." [99]

The crisis that eventually led to the Berlin Airlift first began with several smaller upheavals. In March 1948, the Soviet issued an order restricting military and passenger traffic between Berlin and the Western Occupation Zones. Also, no cargo could leave by rail without express permission of the Soviet commander but even then, they would continue to disrupt road and rail traffic. Then the Currency Crisis happened—Britain and the US introduced the Deutsche Mark in order to stabilize and standardize the currency which the Soviets were debasing. It had gotten to the point where Germans were using cigarettes as currency since the Reichmark became almost worthless. The allies brought in 250 million Deutsche Marks which tipped Stalin's hand leading to their blockade of West Berlin. All traffic in and out of West Berlin was now prevented except for three air corridors that had been earlier agreed upon. Two million people were now effectively cut off from food, fuel and essential supplies. It was the Soviet version of Mao's blockade of Changchun which was occurring at the very same time. The West Berliners, now being predominantly women and children, were expendable pawns in Stalin's effort towards taking over Berlin. [98]

Quick action was taken by the British and American occupation forces to use the designated air corridors. The southern corridor, used by the US, started out from their bases at Weisbaden and Frankfurt (Rhein-Mein), extending for a hundred miles before landing at Berlin's Tempelhof Airport. The British northern route originated from several bases, including Fassberg, Celle, Wunstorf and Finkenwerde then landed in Berlin at Gatow and Tegel airfields. The central corridor was used by both allies for return flights to their respective bases for reloading with more cargo. The quick action, however, would soon transform into a logistical nightmare which required continual tweaking and refinement. As Halvorsen also notes,

> "On my first trip to Berlin, I didn't know what to expect to see when I would meet Germans. However, these last feelings of doubt left me when I landed that first load of 20,000 pounds of flour at Tempelhof Airport. The lead man of the German unloading crew came toward the cockpit with moist eyes and a hand thrust out in friendship. His words of gratitude were unintelligible, but his expression said it all." [99]

> "I asked another pilot how he felt about flying day and night on behalf of the enemy ... the very ones who did their best to kill him as he flew over Berlin in 1944. He shuffled his feet for a moment and then said, 'It feels a lot better to feed them than it does to kill them'. ' Another pilot added, 'I didn't feel good about dropping the bombs. Now maybe I can do something (positive) by delivering the food.'" [99]

Figuring out how much food to send started with the assumption of each person needing 1,900 calories per day, then augmented by the need for protein, vegetables, fresh milk, etc. As winter approached, the summer tonnage no longer was adequate since Berliners started requiring coal to stay warm. They needed sturdy coal sacks to effect transport and distribution, many of which would be pilfered. Different planes had different characteristics and load capacities. To achieve an efficient assembly line of planes coming in, they were "stacked" both vertically and horizontally. If a pilot missed his delivery by overshooting a short runway, he had to return to base so as not to disrupt the arrival of all the other planes. Add to that the fickle weather and difficulties the Soviets sometimes tossed in, it's a wonder the 15-month airlift succeeded. The Soviets had their own doubts, only to be later embarrassed with the operation's success leading to their lifting the blockade. At peak efficiency, a plane was said to land every 45 seconds at Tempelhof Airport. [98]

One day, early in the operation, Lieutenant Halvorsen headed to Tempelhof and while taking photos near the runway, he noticed a group of German kids watching the planes landing. He went over to say hello, using his limited German. Aged between eight and fourteen, Halvorsen would be astonished by their intelligent questions and level of maturity. One girl with melancholy blue eyes, about twelve years old, was their designated spokesperson. She said to him:

> "Almost every one of us here experienced the final battle for Berlin. After your bombers had killed some of our parents, brothers, and sisters, we thought nothing could be worse. But then we saw firsthand the communist system. We've learned so much more since that time. We don't need lectures on freedom. We can walk on both sides of the border (before the wall went up). What you see speaks more strongly than the words you hear or read." [99]

Halvorsen's experience that day with the group of thirty kids bunched behind the airport fence would lead him and many other pilots to initiate Operation Little Vittles. They began dropping candies, gum and chocolates from their own rations, using little parachutes made from handkerchiefs. Before long, American candy companies and stateside volunteer organizations making parachutes would become actively involved. The media took notice and there were numerous requests by American children to become pen pals with the German kids. The Berlin airlift coupled with the Little Vittles operation would become a huge propaganda success story for the Americans, effectively winning the hearts of former enemies while also repudiating communism. [99]

Halvorsen did respond to the letter from young Mercedes explaining not being able to locate her chicken coop from the air. He did say, however, that he sent her a box of goodies by mail. Twenty-three years later, in 1971, a Peter Wild approached now Colonel Halvorsen who had taken over Air Force command of Tempelhof Airport, telling him his wife often spoke about the Chocolate Pilot and candy parachutes. Mercedes Simon Wild, who was a thirty-year-old mother at that time, remembered with fondness what the Americans did many years ago. The Wilds and Halvorsen family would go on to become lifelong friends. [99]

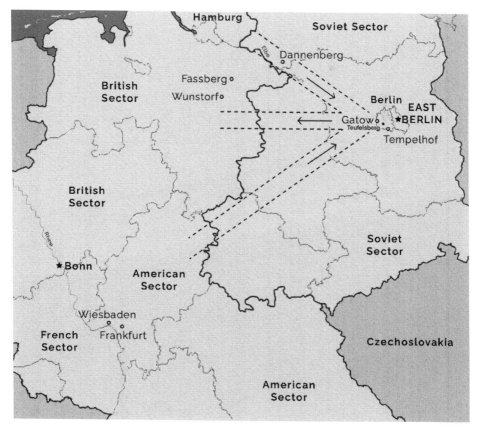

The Berlin Airlift (1948 - 1949)

# Standoff at Toktong Pass

In October 1950, a year after declaring establishment of the People's Republic of China in Beijing's Tiananmen Square, Chairman Mao decided to use his forces to accomplish several objectives. The People's Liberation Army (PLA) was now big, buttressed by a continual influx of rural peasants and Nationalists who had switched loyalties. He believed Tibet to be an integral part of China and while wresting southern China from Nationalist control, Tibet was initially not among the regions involved. The Chairman also wanted Tibet, relying on various historical justifications, whereas the Tibetan's longed to retain their cherished independence. The Communist forces, unsurprisingly, would overwhelm the undermanned Tibetan Army which, from Mao's perspective, "liberated" the vast region to become a part of China. [10]

Another decision for Mao to make in late 1950 was whether or not to enter the conflict that was taking place in Korea. His People's Liberation Army (PLA), while strong, still had problems holding over from the civil war. Problems which included China's rampant hyperinflation, need for domestic consolidation and still lingering anti-communist resistance in the south. He was also due to release 1.5 million soldiers from active military service. The dilemma was whether to enter the Korean War to support a communist ally while confronting a technologically superior foe. A foe which had atomic destruction capacity which China lacked. During that fall, Mao massed his troops in Manchuria just in case, while he monitored developments with interest and later with concern. [10, 11]

Stalin didn't want a war with the Americans, whom he was already tussling with in Berlin, but he had few reservations about acting in a supporting role. Mao, however, harbored more immediate concerns. Manchuria was China's industrial center in a largely rural populated country and several of his hydro-electric plants sat right along the border with North Korea. He needed a buffer, one large enough and far away from American bombers. The "tripwire" in his mind, would be a UN incursion across the 38th Parallel, indicating an intent to push all the way to the Chinese border. That line was crossed, and 250,000 soldiers, which Mao renamed the People's Volunteer Army, began pouring across the Yalu on October 19, 1950. [15]

The Korean War actually began that July with Kim Il Sung, previously installed to power by Stalin, now attempting to unify the entire Korea peninsula under communist rule. The undermanned and ill-equipped American and South Korean forces were easily pushed back to the Pusan Perimeter, a small pocket at the southeastern tip of the peninsula. When American forces were quickly reconstituted, an amphibious operation spearheaded by with the 1st Marine Division landed at Inchon, 17 miles west of Seoul on September 15. Seoul would be retaken later that month, followed by the UN force's first incursion across the 38th Parallel. [15}

On October 26, the 1st Marine Division, having completed their mission of taking Seoul, re-boarded US Navy ships to debark at Wonsan which sat on the peninsula's east side, 100 miles above the 38th Parallel. By the middle of the following month, they travelled northward, first reaching Hagaru—entry point to Chosin Reservoir—as part of X Corps' plan as the right pincer of UN force's drive to the Yalu. Leaving their headquarters and 1st Regiment in Hagaru, the division advanced another 14 miles up the MSR, a dirt mountain road to Yudom-ni, on the reservoir's west side. It was there that the drive was suddenly stopped in its tracks by 120,000 attacking Chinese soldiers making up eight full-strength divisions. The Marines of the 5th and 7th Regiments along with the 11th artillery adopted a defensive posture, essentially reverting to survival mode. They hunkered down to fight the Chinese onslaught while enduring climate hardships imposed by minus 20-degree weather. [13]

## Part One (1947-1954)

The 1st Marine Division is a storied outfit—the Corps' oldest and most decorated division—that was in Korea and being commanded by Major General Oliver Smith. Smith, a tall, thin and somewhat unassuming man who didn't quite strike most as the gung-ho commander of fighting Marines; however, looks were deceiving. The Marine Corps was and is still well sprinkled with self-effacing men like Smith whose root core reeked of a sublime toughness: a "let's finish the job" mentality. With neither a raised voice or uttered curse, General Smith was a calculating strategist, carefully weighing all probable risks of loss in equal measure to usual Corps aggressiveness. Given the faults and vanities of his Army superiors such as McArthur and Generals Almond and Willoughby, Smith stood in stark contrast. Almond was Smith's superior and an appointee of McArthur. The Marines felt Almond was too admiring of McArthur and needlessly reckless in order to appease his boss. Military pundits in Washington and Korea, believed the brawl was really the 1st Marine Division's to fight and that General Smith was indeed the right man for the job. [13]

As the Marines were marching up the Main Supply Route (MSR) towards Yudom-ni, Fox company of the 7th Marines was informed they were to stop midway and "babysit" Fox Hill near Toktong Pass. Little did they appreciate how much the Chinese really wanted Fox Hill as it was the MSR's chokepoint, the only road leading into and out of the Chosin Reservoir. Giving up Fox Hill would permit a dangerous encirclement and condemn the 5th and 7th Marine Regiments to annihilation. [12, 13]

Yet another unassuming Marine officer, Captain William Barber, was Fox's new company commander. As a tall man with an unremarkable face sporting an odd-shaped nose and thinning brown hair, thirty-year old Barber struck most people as having the look of an actuary or accountant. Yet the studious Kentuckian was also a star athlete at Morehead State and a decorated World War II veteran. His baptism of fire was as a platoon commander with the 1st Parachute Regiment of the 5th Marine Division on Iwo Jima. The same outfit as Anthony Poshepny. Poshepny, better known as "Tony Poe", would later join the CIA as a trainer of Tibetan freedom fighters and achieve notoriety during the Secret War in Laos. [12]

Barber was appalled at the appearance of Fox Company when he took over command prior to the long march north. He felt the men looked like Pancho Villa bandits and wanted them to shave, clean their weapons and prepare for an early morning conditioning hike. He also would institute daily rifle practice to improve their marksmanship skills. The men groused and complained behind their new commander's back but he didn't care. At one point, he was just like them before being commissioned; also, he knew that "you're not a Marine unless you're bitching about something or another." Barber got the company in snap-to shape in relatively short order. He had recently read a translated copy of the enemy's manifesto, titled "Military Lessons" that Mao had given to his own soldiers. It acknowledged American superiority in tanks, planes and artillery. However, it went on to say, "Their infantry is weak. These men are afraid to die, and will neither press home a bold attack nor will they defend to the death." Barber set the book down, thinking "Nope... not my Marines." [12]

Another captured Chinese document stated:

> "Soon we will meet the American Marines in battle and destroy them. Kill these Marines as you would kill snakes in your homes!"

The first night on Fox Hill, all hell was about to break loose. While it was still daylight, Barber ordered the men to dig in, after assigning perimeters and fields of fire for his three platoon's, machine gun teams and mortar squad. He had them dig foxholes in the frozen terrain. The grousing intensity soon increased, not so much directed at Barber but at the ground itself. It was akin to chipping away at concrete. He would also need a command post established and tent area for his medical corpsmen.

At just after 2 am, a ghostly mob of white clad Chinese soldiers were seen scurrying in the near distance, followed by a growing cacophony of noise, including bugles, gunfire, explosions, whistles, and even clanging cymbals as one of the Marines yelled out, "HERE THEY COME!" Corporal Page, without hesitation, opened up his heavy machine gun. Raking the Chinese with multiple bursts, like a scythe threshing a field of wheat, he cut them down. As Barber scrambled out of his sleeping bag, rushing to lace up his boots, the mortar team was racing up the hill with their tubes, plates and ammo. The Chinese soon figured out Page's position by the red tracer rounds he was using and focused much of their fire in that direction. Use of tracers were largely curtailed after that first night. The Battle of Fox Hill had begun! [12]

The attacking Chinese lobbed "potato mashers", which were grenades having a wooden handle for ease of throwing. The Marines were directing their M-1 and Browning Automatic Rifle (BAR) fire correctly but the enemy didn't appear to be dropping. It seemed like the bullets just weren't penetrating the heavily quilted Chinese uniforms. Someone in the Fox ranks wisely shouted, "AIM FOR THEIR HEADS!"

Some Marine positions were quickly over-run that night, with several of the most forward Marines bayoneted while they were still in their sleeping bags. The Chinese were dropping but yet more still came in waves of fifty men each. They began creating multiple holes in Fox Company's carefully designed perimeter. One Marine named Private Gomez yelled for his foxhole mate to hand him some ammo. When the guy didn't respond, Gomez glanced over at his face and saw he'd been shot through the left eye. [12]

The four members of Corporal Koone's fire team stood up together to give the commies a taste of concentrated fire.... but nothing happened. It seems all their rifles misfired due to firing pins being frozen. This even happened to Koone's BAR. Some of the grenades the Marines tossed turned out to be duds, being surplus stock held over from World War II. The madness went on for four hours until dawn. In the morning light, Chinese dead and wounded were seen carpeting the hillsides, with their cries, prayers and singing of death songs noticeably heard. One of the Chinese battlefield tactics was to play dead until a Marine approached and that was when he would suddenly pop up and kill him. Barber felt this to be an appalling violation of accepted rules of warfare, so he ordered his men to shoot fallen Chinese soldiers, whether they appeared dead or alive. Within the foxholes and medical tent, the corpsmen were frantically busy tending to the wounded and stacking up the dead. [12, 13]

On successive days, the night attacks continued, sometimes moderately but usually more intense. During daytime, enemy snipers plied their trade with particular focus on the Fox Company machine gunners. One night, Private Cafferata grew weary of throwing back potato mashers that were being lobbed towards his foxhole. When the volume increased, he began hitting many back with his entrenching tool as if he was in batting practice. However, his luck would run its course as one blew up just as he released it. His throwing hand was left a bloody mess, but Cafferata continued the fight by firing his rifle, wondering whether he had semi-pro ball potential. Assuming, of course, that he made it through all this alive.

One Marine had the distasteful task of having to identify his close friend, Corporal Farley, who had his face blown away. Farley's wife had recently sent him a care package of gin disguised as olive juice, which Farley shared with all his buddies. Morphine syrettes carried by all medical corpsmen were also known to freeze in the bitter cold weather and required thawing first by placing under the tongue or in the crotch area. Cutting off the clothing to attend to a wound risked gangrene and frostbite. The Corpsmen said if there was one good thing to result from the below zero cold, it was that many wounds would cease to bleed. Also, corpses didn't smell. By the next day, Fox Company would be down below two thirds strength. Supplies, especially ammunition and fresh batteries, were soon being airdropped. Runners sent to retrieve the packages became adept at zig zagging to avoid being picked off by Chinese snipers. [12, 13]

On the following day, Captain Barber was hit—a bullet ricocheted off Lieutenant McCarthy's rifle stock and plowed right into Barber's pelvis. He plugged the hole as best as he could and refused corpsmen assistance as he limped off towards the med tent, holding onto McCarthy. The human wave attacks were essentially over but moderate rifle fire continued, as did the incessant daytime sniping. The corpsmen patched and splinted Barber as best they could and he hobbled around using a tree limb as a crutch, barking orders to his men. The 7th Marines Regimental commander, Colonel Litzenberg, called Barber on the radio asking if he wanted to give up the hill and fight his way back to Hagaru. Barber's thinking was 'now that we got the hill, we might as well keep it.' Accordingly, he responded, "We will hold, Sir." [12]

By the sixth day, Barber's wound had gotten worse and he now required a couple of Marines to carry him around on a stretcher. The shattered bone was causing an infection which soon advanced down his leg. He still made sure he didn't neglect his perimeter inspections while being ferried around on a stretcher... being sure of also telling his men how proud he was of them. In the morning, he got a call from Lt Colonel Ray Davis, who had been leading a battalion sent overland from Yudam-ni to relieve Fox Company. By that time, Fox Company was down to 85 "effectives" from a starting roster of 235 Marines. Barber ordered a general cleanup of the hill, including taking his dead Marines down to the MSR for transport. Throughout the hillsite still lay over a thousand dead Chinese soldiers, including many who had been dragged by Marines to act as sand bags around their foxholes. Unlike the Marines, the Chinese Army made no attempt to evacuate their wounded from the field of battle. Fighting for Mao, if you can't walk out, you're simply left there to die.

Captain Barber turned over command of Fox Company to Lieutenant Abell as he was carefully loaded into a jeep for transport to Hagaru and eventual evacuation aboard an awaiting hospital ship. The remnants of Fox Company straggled down the MSR as best they could. As they closed in on Hagaru, many got into lockstep, a strained but earnest attempt to keep in marching formation. Someone started quietly humming the Marine Corps' Hymn and by the time they entered Hagaru, all were singing it out loud.

In 1952, Captain William Barber would be awarded the Congressional Medal of Honor for his leadership in holding Fox Hill under severe conditions and against insurmountable odds. He died of cancer in 2002 at age eighty-two. At his funeral service, one side of the church was filled with veterans of Fox Company. On the other sat family, friends and retired servicemen. Just as the ceremony was about to began, Barber's only son, John, got up, kissed his mother, and proudly strode across the aisle to sit with his father's men. [12]

Several lessons were learned or should have been learned from the Korean War experience. The first and foremost lesson involved intelligence: its gathering, analysis and management both by the CIA as well as the military. It's as much an art as it is science and results may not always come out as expected but when it came to Korean War, the neglect and mismanagement of intelligence can and did result in casualties. Simply put, people died. America had suffered a similar experience with the sneak attack on Pearl Harbor, carried out on December 7, 1941.

MacArthur would not allow the CIA to have a representative in Japan, similar to as he had done with the OSS during his Southwest Pacific Command in World War II. His intelligence staff listened intently but only to him, providing only the necessary information which supported his agenda and viewpoint. Anything contradictory was not allowed or was watered down, thereby allowing him to maintain overall control as he saw it fit. His staff, particularly Major General Charles Willoughby, acting G-2/Intelligence, reinforced MacArthur's whims and mindset. In June 1950, Willoughby advised MacArthur that the North Koreans would not invade the south but on June 25, the communists invaded. In the fall of that year, Willoughby neither believed nor attempted to confirm that Chinese communist troops had entered North Korea. Captured Chinese prisoners were summarily dismissed by General Willoughby as being "advisors" without any further investigation being conducted. When several Chinese divisions were found in Korea, he asserted they were neither full strength nor combat ready. He even doctored an intelligence report that had been sent to his boss. That same report encouraged MacArthur to proceed to the Yalu by stating communist Chinese strength was only a tenth of what it really was. [15]

Aside from Marine Corps' frustrations with Army Central Command, many army veterans from that period also believed General Willoughby's failure to admit the validity of the evidence and suggest a reorientation of allied forces to properly address the Chinese threat was responsible for many of the disasters that followed.

## Part One (1947-1954)

While MacArthur disallowed the CIA to operate in Tokyo, the agency nonetheless did conduct its own research as to Chinese capabilities and intention when it came to Korean conflict. Between July and November 1950, its Office of Reports and Estimates (ORE) produced a series of ten memorandums for the CIA Director addressing "Chinese Intentions." Their research was largely based on gathering human intelligence and their Foreign Broadcast Information Service listening to radio broadcasts from the USSR, China, and other Far East countries. News reports mentioned Chinese troop movements heading northwards into Manchuria and along the Korean border. In ORE's September 1950 report, coming out a month or so prior to China's actual incursion, it was stated that there was "increased buildup of Chinese military strength in Manchuria with possibly 400,000 Communist soldiers already massed there or soon to arrive." The report concluded: "the stage has been set for some form of Chinese Communist intervention or participation in the Korean War." [15]

Interestingly, in a formal report that was sent from CIA Director Walter Bedell Smith to the President on October 12, 1950, it was said that there were "no convincing indication of an actual Chinese intention to resort to full-scale intervention in Korea." Even when Chinese troops did enter North Korea, it seemed the CIA analysts failed to grasp the significance of what was really happening.

Worsening the intelligence situation, was a meeting President Truman had on Wake Island on October 15, 1950, wherein MacArthur commented that the "troops will be home by Christmas." When Truman asked MacArthur about China, the general stated that "they would not intervene in the war." However, MacArthur had already set his mind to charging ahead to the Yalu and taking the whole of Korea, intelligence be damned. On October 19, four days later, the People's Volunteer Army of 260,000 men would cross over the border into North Korea. [15]

Note that Chinese Premier Zhou En-Lai had issued a warning September 30th that "China would not tolerate UN forces crossing the 38th Parallel and would not stand aside were that to happen." Then three days later, when speaking to Indian Ambassador Panikkar, he again stated that if non-Korean troops crossed the 38th, "China would send troops into Korea." MacArthur's staff, as well as the CIA, knew about these warnings yet they chose to ignore them. They appeared to be giving no weight, whatsoever, to what was known on whether or not the Chinese were going to invade.

Another take-away from the war pertained to military strategy and the fighting capability of the Chinese forces. Chinese soldiers were taller than their North Korean counterparts and had years of fighting experience borne from the bloody civil war. They certainly weren't pushovers. In fact, it's said the South Korean military carried a healthy fear of going up against PLA fighters. They were relatively well clothed for winter fighting and utilized camouflage well. That said, they suffered from high rates frostbite as much as the Americans did. A Chinese soldier's arsenal included a menagerie of small arms, including British Lee-Enfields, Russian burp guns, American Springfields, and Thompson machine guns.... the latter courtesy of US weapons confiscated from Chiang Kai-shek's forces during the civil war. They had no artillery or tanks to speak of but did use 81mm mortars. Any air assets were provided in limited form by the Soviets who preferred to use their own planes and pilots. In fact, the world's first jet vs jet dogfight occurred early on in the war between an F-86 Sabre and a MiG-15. The Soviet in the MiG won. [15]

As far as strategy, the Chinese had, by the late 1940s, adopted mobile large-unit warfare in lieu of the guerrilla tactics commonly used in previous years of the Chinese Civil War. Siege warfare as used by Lin Bao in Changchun had been shown to be effective but in Korea, Lin Bao wasn't in charge and the old methods no longer applied. Marshall Peng Dehuai, personally chosen by Mao, was up against a more technologically advanced army which had air superiority. Peng's advantage, as he perceived it, was with the fighting spirit of his politically indoctrinated soldiers. He felt that on a man-to-man basis, his soldiers were superior fighters to the Americans.... and he had multitudes of them in his ranks.

## Part One (1947-1954)

One strategy that was used was the "V" or Venus Flytrap maneuver where his troops would engage the enemy, feign weakness to draw him in deeper and then have each side or flank close up the trap. This was used by small and large units alike. Other methods simply involved various forms of envelopment. Knowing that the US had command of the skies, Peng was careful to only move his troops around at night, also avoiding the use of roads. As shown at Chosin Reservoir, they also attacked en masse at night, while setting out snipers to pick off the enemy during daytime. In those days, before night vision goggles and night attack fighter jets, this proved to be an effective light infantry strategy. With the exception of maybe Nationalist soldiers who had surrendered and joined Mao's forces, most die-hard PLA fighters could be fanatical, particularly if armed commissars were following behind. Prior Nationalists were typically less zealous and also more likely to divulge vital information to the Americans when captured. [15]

What kept the Chinese from victory was the continual difficulty in keeping their troops supplied. They couldn't move supplies by truck during daylight due to American air superiority, so their chief logistician, Hung She Te, came up with a next best solution using porters and oxcarts. The need for constructing and maintaining viable resupply routes was also a recognized necessity in China's takeover of Tibet. It would yet again become a familiar problem for Ho Chi Minh to deal with years later during the Vietnam War. In Korea, it was said that once a Chinese unit depleted its allotment of ammunition, it had to quit the battlefield until it was resupplied. Hu Seng, Peng's deputy, also noted that it was relatively easy to track enemy troop movements as US communications security during the war was often lax. Finally, Peng believed the Americans 'mobility advantage in general allowed them to escape possible defeat time and again. [15]

Of course, as a last resort, the United States also had the atomic bomb coupled with the wherewithal to effect delivery.

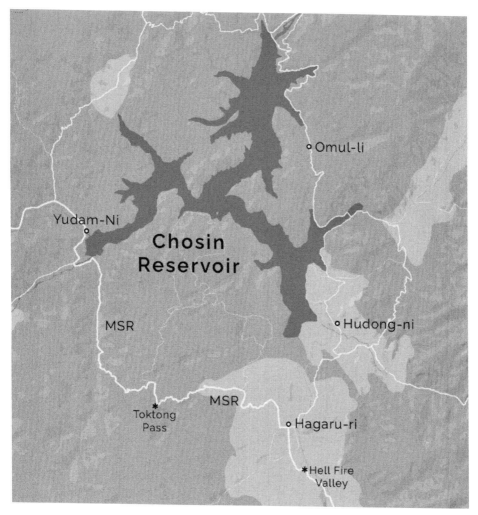

Chosin Reservoir, Korea (1950)

# Downey and Fecteau

Late 1952 and 1953 were the years the authors were born, being brought into a brave new world still riding vestiges of post-war euphoria. We were the "leading edge" baby boomers, born between 1946 and 1955 who would later come of age during the turbulent Vietnam War. Post-war economic expansion brought with it promises in education, prosperity and health. Dr. Jonas Salk had just developed the polio vaccine, the dreaded scourge of every parent, and average life expectancy was increasing steadily. Eisenhower had just been elected by a resounding majority and there was good reason to look forward to the coming decade. Despite that cause for optimism, the US was just coming out of a war in Korea against communism, the new nemesis on the block. The resulting Cold War would continue for decades, influencing regime changes, alliances and a prolonged strategic arms buildup. The fledgling CIA, founded just five years previously, would be challenged in a wartime setting... starting first with the Korean Peninsula in the winter of November 1952.

The selected drop zone was Chang Pai Mountain, about twenty-five miles north of the North Korean border. After three cold, bumpy hours in the air, the olive drab C-47 transport finally reached its destination right around midnight. C-47s then were the real workhorses of the Civil Air Transport (CAT)—the airline used by the agency when secrecy was the order of the day. Almost on cue, Downey and Fecteau received the awaited signal from the ground and proceeded to push out bundled crates of food from the side cargo door. [6, 37]

It was not only food they shoved out but boxes of specialized equipment needed to perform aerial extraction of the agent waiting patiently below. The ground pickup technique was tricky and dangerous, having been practiced by the agents only a few times; however, everything had to work exactly as expected. The Fulton Skyhook system involved an extractee on the ground wearing a harness "jacket" which was attached to a line strung up on two poles he had planted into the ground. The plane would then make a low-level pass at near stall speed—at about 60 knots—to snag the line from a hook extending out the rear of the plane. Once hooked and airborne, Downey and Fecteau would use the onboard winch to pull the extracted man into the plane. Pilots Schwartz and Snoddy had practiced the maneuver a few months previously but this now was the real thing. An actual mission about to place during dead of night in Manchuria's wintery hinterland. [6]

Everyone became more nervous after spotting several men scurrying around below in the moonlit landscape and another who had strapped on the harness jacket. The poles and line appeared to be correctly set up. One rehearsal flyby was already done and now it was time, for the real McCoy... the actual extraction maneuver.

As the plane came in low and slow once again, white sheets were suddenly ripped away, revealing two anti-aircraft guns that had been hidden. "BLAM BLAM" was the sound that followed as they immediately commenced firing on both sides of the plane. The C-47 was being ambushed by a concentration of crossfire ripping violently into the fuselage. The guns were quickly joined by a chorus of small arms fire from men suddenly appearing out of hiding. The pilots were frantically yelling commands as Schwartz tried desperately to keep the plane's nose up but the aircraft stalled and quickly crashed into a nearby grove of trees. The small arms shooting had been mostly directed at the cockpit which was now set ablaze. Downey and Fecteau would be violently tossed around but surprisingly were left unscathed due to their heavily layered clothing. [6, 37]

## Part One (1947-1954)

> "Dick, quickly.... we need to check on the pilots!"
> Downey yelled as he rushed towards the front.

The fuselage, at that point, had broken into two pieces and blustery wind mixed with snow pushed its way inside.

> "Shit, I can't open this damn door! Give me a hand,"
> Fecteau implored.

Try as they might, even after using a makeshift crowbar, the cockpit door was jammed too tight. Suddenly, sounds were no longer being heard from behind the door. The flames had gotten bigger, whipping at them while they were still frantically trying to pry the door open. It became obvious the time had come to save themselves as the plane was close to exploding.

Bullets were occasionally pinging off and sometimes puncturing the plane's cladding but there were now enough jagged openings to the outside for them jump out. No sooner had they hit the ground then they were quickly engulfed by angry shouting Communist soldiers. CAT pilots Schwartz and Snoddy died upon impact or horribly while trapped inside the burning cockpit. It dawned on Downey later that, in contrast to the pilots, he and Fecteau were intended to be taken alive. On that fateful night of November 29, 1952, the long ordeal of CIA agents John T. Downey and Richard J. Fecteau was about to begin. [6]

Downey and Fecteau were considered a tad young by CIA standards but their other qualities were what impressed agency recruiters. They were both New Englanders with Downey graduating from Yale and Fecteau from Boston College. Downey signed up June 1951, shortly after graduation, followed by Fecteau a few months later. They were bright, ambitious, patriotic and athletic, each being a member of their respective football teams. Just the type of men the CIA wanted to groom for Far East clandestine service.

As Downey would relate many years later: "A visiting agency official, told interested Yale students that they might be"parachuting behind enemy lines to help set up a resistance network. Hey, that was as glamorous as anything we could have hoped for. A large number of the outstanding people in my senior class applied." The guerrilla exploits of the Office of Strategic Services (OSS) in World War II was still fresh and fascinated many of the young men. The Office of Planning Coordination (OPC) section was pitched by the recruiter to be the new outfit, the "red hot" arm of the CIA. The agency was quite selective, accepting only six of the thirty at Yale who applied. Even then, half of the candidates washed out before training was completed. Downey underwent six months of paramilitary training, including a stint at Fort Benning, Georgia. Training would later move to Camp Peary near Williamsburg, Virginia in what the CIA later called "The Farm" and Fecteau would be one of the first to attend "The Farm" when it opened in July 1952. Other agency notables who attended the first or second classes at Camp Peary included Tony Poe, Bill Lair, Pat Landry and Jack Shirley. [6]

The night in question was a CIA mission called "Staroma" with Downey tasked to establish a resistance network in Jilin. The capital of this Manchuria province just happened to be Changchun where Mao's starvation siege took place just four years earlier. The flight that night originated out of Seoul and was intended to extract an anti-Communist infiltrator carrying classified documents. He had been part of a four-man team selected by Downey to be inserted into the Chinese mainland several months previously. Like many of such guerrilla teams insertions, they went foul or were never heard from again. Downey's particular group had apparently been compromised by Communists to set up an ambush. All four people aboard the C-47 were now considered missing in action and a cover story was concocted by the CIA to explain what happened. Nothing would be heard about the matter until late 1954, following the announcement of a trial verdict on Downey and Fecteau. They had been held in separate prisons almost the entire two years. [6, 37]

Under the stress of frequent solitary confinement and mental harassment, Downey and Fecteau divulged their involvement with the CIA and confessed. Of course, the Chinese already knew or likely suspected this but they wanted the US government to acknowledge it. Chinese Prime Minister Zhou Enlai suggested that he was open to discussing terms for the release of the Americans but Secretary of State John Foster Dulles forbade any negotiations on such "false charges." Foster was also able to persuade President Eisenhower not to provide China an apology which would have perhaps released the two agents. Thus, both Downey and Fecteau festered in Chinese prison, despite being given a chance for freedom in 1954 and again in 1957. [6]

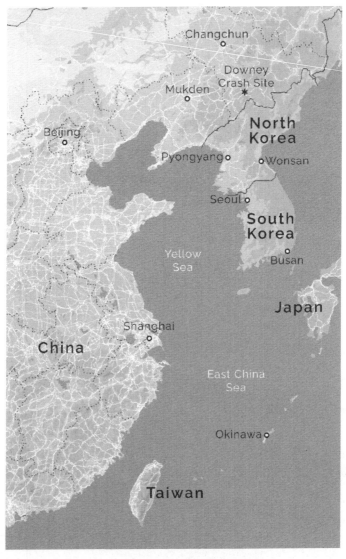

East Asia and the Korean Peninsula (1950s)

# Pirates of Taiwan Straits

The original story started way back in October 1633 as the Battle of Liaoluo Bay was nearing conclusion. The bay sits on the south side of Quemoy Island, itself being a stone's throw off the coast of mainland China. The Dutch East India Company fleet made a surprise attack at the nearby island of Amoy which routed the ships commanded by Zheng Zhilong, a noted pirate in the Taiwan Straits. Zhilong's junks were a sight to behold. They'd been refitted to accommodate 36 large size cannons instead of the usual eight smaller ones. Even Hans Putmans, the Dutch admiral, often marveled at the ingenuity of what Zhilong had done. The change was for naught as Putmans caught the junks off-guard, having only workers aboard at the time instead of the usual battle crewmen. They would have none of this fight and promptly jumped overboard. With the fleet now devastated, the Dutch roamed the offshore islands and coast with their pirate collaborators with impunity. Zhilong would renounce his own pirate days and rebuild his fleet bestowing his allegiance now to the Ming government. [5, 27]

Desperate for revenge, Zhilong would lure the Dutch into Liaoluo Bay, on the south side of Quemoy Island, and surrounded Putnams' vessels to prevent escape. Zhilong ordered his sailors to ignore Putnams' pirate collaborators who were trying to escape. He wanted the "Red Hair Barbarians": as the Dutch were often referred to at the time. Zhilong knew he was no match in a cannon duel with the Dutch so he turned several his warjunks into "fireships" by sending them aflame with crew and cannon, headlong into the Dutch vessels. The crews all carried long bamboo poles used to propel the burning ships forward and then to vault off at the very last moment. The plan worked. Most of Putmans' warships were either sunk or captured leading to a decisive Ming victory and Zheng Zhilong's everlasting fame. [27]

Jumping ahead three hundred years to October 1949, Quemoy Island (also known as Kinmen) would soon be the scene of yet another epic skirmish, the Battle of Kuningtou. As Mao's army kept Chiang Kai-shek on the run in late 1949 and his forces began retreating to Taiwan, a substantial garrison of Nationalist troops remained on Quemoy and Matsu Islands as a sort of rear guard. Quemoy measuring 10 by 5 miles lies only 6 miles off the mainland coast and is 115 miles distant from Taiwan. Like many of the islands dotting the Chinese coast near the Taiwan Straits, this was really a big rock, not having so much as even a tree to speak of. But this rock would take on strategic significance. [5]

Chiang's Kuomintang army had been beaten by Mao's People Liberation Army (PLA) in battle after battle and there was expectation of yet another major attack, first on Quemoy and then to take over Taiwan. PLA General Ye Fei brought forth two assault waves totaling 20,000 light infantry being transported by two hundred junks and wooden fishing boats. Fei's expectation was that the island would be easily taken in a matter of three days. The over confidence resulting also from poor intel would, however, lead to their demise. General Fei thought the garrison defending Quemoy was much smaller and largely made up of low morale conscripts. Chiang's forces, however, were well prepared for the onslaught with installed beach obstacles, land mines, and several tank companies with American M5A1 tanks waiting in earnest. They even called in Nationalist B-26 bombers for air support when needed. It was a classic lesson on how not to conduct an amphibious assault which led to the entire PLA force being killed or captured. The Battle of Kuningtou would go down in history as a tremendous morale boost for Chiang's beleaguered forces. Crushing the PLA's chance of taking Taiwan and defeating the Nationalists once and for all, Quemoy would become a recurring flashpoint in the years to come. [5, 19]

Up to the middle of the 20th century, guerrilla pirates and Communists were still sailing Chinese junks with their oversized flat masts as they had in centuries past.

Large-masted junks, the sea vessel of choice, were actually said by a noted historian to be one of the most efficient of ship designs. Some raiders' junks would fly the black skull & crossbones flag under the Nationalist ensign which was given to them by the Americans. The guerrillas 'junks were often larger and better armed than their Communist counterparts, sporting mounted 20mm cannons and .50 cal machine guns. Over time, more vessels would become motorized and have their masts repurposed for other uses. [5]

Sea worthiness, speed and mobility of junks become primary factors easily trumping the need for more firepower. Smaller sampan boats were towed behind to get guerrillas ashore so as to prevent accidental beaching of the larger junks. As in the old days, the coastal tides could be tricky changing by as much as twenty feet during a cycle. Care also had to be taken into account for the annual typhoon season. In a sea battle, when it appeared that the Communists had reinforcements well on the way, the guerrilla junks quickly withdrew. It was typical guerrilla tactics whether it be on land or at sea. [5]

The Nationalist guerrillas and their CIA mentors themselves would often take on aspects reminiscent of the pirates of yesteryear, including a group of unique characters. Most famous was the "One-Eyed Dragon", real name LtCol. Ed Hamilton, who was the Western Enterprises, Inc (WEI) commander on Quemoy Island. Ed had been a battalion commander during the D-Day landing in France when he lost an eye. He would command the respect and friendship of those who knew him and took the nickname with his usual good humor. When playing poker, Ed was known to sometimes place his glass eye strategically on the table as if peering at the other players' cards. He contended that it gave his game an edge. Despite occasional quirkiness, the Dragon was an inspirational commander. [5, 19]

Other personalities included "Texas Jim" Creacy, who was seldom seen without his ten-gallon hat. On the pistol range, he'd practice with his ivory handled revolvers carved with dragons that he purchased in Hong Kong. Texas Jim was a noted specialist in communications. Not to be outdone, there were also their Nationalist compatriots like "Fat Wang." Wang Shang-chuan was an over-sized bear of a man with a glint in his eye and a quip or joke ready to burst forth at any moment. Make no mistake, however, Fat Wang was every bit an accomplished warrior and leader. He respected his men and they returned the favor.

The Americans also included "Major Bob" Barrow on temporary loan from the US Marines, which would begin replacing the OSS veterans. Barrow was more the no-nonsense type and brought the expertise of having led guerrilla teams right in Mao's backyard. He had recently distinguished himself in Korea where he was awarded the Silver Star and Navy Cross. In later years, a now General Barrow would go on to serve as the 27th Commandant of the Marine Corps. Several raiding parties also took aboard Roger McCarthy for his logistics and communications expertise. McCarthy would, in the late 1950s, train Tibetan freedom fighters on Saipan and also at Camp Hale, Colorado along with Frank Holober, author of "Raiders of the China Coast." [5]

It was work and often dangerous but not without its occasional lighter moments. One time, the Dragon arranged for a combat newsreel to be filmed of one of the raids to show the American public back home the fighting spirit of the guerrilla fighters:

> "Hey Jackson, can you film the operation of our raid this Friday?" (Dragon showing him his WEI movie camera) "I assume you know how to operate this, right?"
>
> "Yea, sure.... no problem," Jackson Hsiang, the camp interpreter replied.

Jackson, the volunteer camera man, was not only new but also apparently skittish in a combat environment full of explosions and flying bullets. Therefore, during filming, he wouldn't always point the camera in the proper direction where the action was. When the men anxiously viewed the first showing after the raid, they noticed that most of the attention in the filming was on civilians... including fifty feet of film devoted solely to the antics of pot belly pigs scurrying around. Needless to say, the Dragon was quite unhappy despite the humorous uproar shared amongst the rest of the men. [5]

Western Enterprises (WEI) was a CIA cover organization in support of the anti-communist island guerrillas. They'd provide training, intelligence gathering, weapons, airdrops of supplies and all manner of logistical support to Nationalist forces during their offensive efforts against Mao's forces. The Military Assistance Advisory Group (MAAG) was started that same year as Western would have its operations restricted to assisting with the defense of Taiwan. As was typical, CIA cover organizations such as Western would be kept secret under the guise of "plausible deniability" whereas MAAG was military staffed and operated, usually being not so secretive. Western was incorporated in February 1951 by Frank Brick and headquartered in Pittsburgh. A former lawyer with the 90th Division, Brick had worked with William "Wild Bill" Donovan, head of the OSS. Another 90th Division alumni, Ed Hamilton, the One-Eyed Dragon, would be appointed as Western's secretary-treasurer. [19]

Western Enterprises found the need to change practices and tactics from time to time as circumstances dictated. Early on, the routine of flying over the mainland and dropping anti-communist leaflets began to provide marginal results at best. The communists responded with the false news that Chiang and the Americans were involved with biological warfare agents and that touching "contaminated" leaflets was to be avoided at all costs.

One of the primary objectives of the raiding was to divert Mao's attention and hopefully some of his combat divisions, from the Korean conflict. He didn't take the bait, however. For the guerrilla effort, there would soon be no more quick drops and marches into the mainland interior. Now, hit-and-run coastal raids were called out using mobile guerrilla teams. Teams were organized on short notice with the date and destination kept tightly under wraps until launch of the operation. There were communist spies almost everywhere, including amongst recent evacuees to Taiwan and fishermen on the many islands. In later years, use of five-hundred man raiding battalions also proved to be ineffective, particularly when guerrillas were no longer fighting local militia, conscripts and old men but rather Mao's seasoned troops now transferred south after the Korean Armistice. After that signing in July 1953, Western Enterprises and their Taiwanese allies would experience diminishing returns with the outcomes of their island and coastal raiding. [5, 19]

Operating concurrently with Western Enterprises operations was the CIA's Third Force concept. Seemingly duplicative in many respects to Western's mission, the Third Force idea sprung forth in late 1949, about the same time of that epic battle with General Fei on Quemoy. CIA agents led by Alfred Cox would scour the mainland looking for commanders to fight against Mao but who also were not allied with Chiang Kai-shek. CIA agents were said to be distributing money "by the bushel" before finding the ex-Nationalist deputy Chief of Staff, Cai Wenzhi, to lead the effort. A 1949 poll in the US had found that Americans favored neither the Communists nor the Nationalists, but rather another alternative, hence a third force. It really wasn't a new concept, as there were third force movements active in France, Germany, Vietnam as well as in China during the past.

The Korean War created a sense of urgency to actively explore this option and the CIA's covert action arm, the Office of Policy Coordination (OPC), was tasked with getting things off the ground by setting up both the Free China Movement and the Fighting League. It was based largely in Hong Kong and it would put a lot of people on the CIA payroll using unvouchered funds. Guerrilla teams would be air dropped onto the Chinese mainland, usually never to be heard from again. Friendly resistance pockets for them to link up with were unreachable but more likely nonexistent. One of these failed missions was the debacle involving agents Downey and Fecteau's capture in Manchuria in late November 1952. [19]

Much of the money and effort was also expended to keep Third Force secret from Chiang Kai-shek and the American China Lobby who naturally opposed the idea given, its commensurate dilution of US support for the Nationalist forces. The CIA finally ended up losing hope in the project, by pulling the plug in 1954 and shifted its full support back to the Nationalists. In 1953, Western Enterprises would limit its emphasis strictly to intelligence gathering and by September

1954, this OPC construct would also be gone. Both programs' demise came within a year after signing of the Korean Armistice and about when the communists started their shelling of Quemoy Island... precipitating the First Taiwan Crisis. [19]

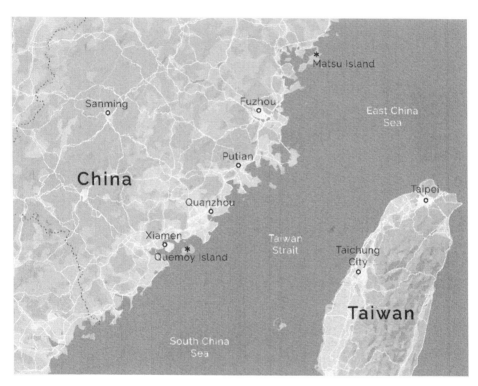

Taiwan, Quemoy and Matsu Islands (1950s)

# Jack in Korea

If "covert renaissance man" was an accepted term, Tony Poe would have a valid claim to its ownership rights. As an 18-year-old, Poe joined the Marine Corps, initially with the later disbanded 2nd parachute Battalion and then to fight with the 5th Marine Division in February 1945 on Iwo Jima. As a sergeant, he was wounded in the leg and eventually recovered only to be discharged that November to attend San Jose State University. Following graduation in 1950, Poe joined the CIA as part of its first class held at Camp Peary, Virginia when it opened its doors July 1952. Another notable in that first class was Richard Fecteau, the agent shot down and captured by Chinese in November. By early 1953, Tony Poe would experience his first CIA assignment while working under Major John Singlaub.

John Singlaub worked at the US Military Liaison Mission in Mukden, Manchuria for three years after World War II, presumably starting after the Soviets left in May 1946. He reported on the Chinese Civil War and then went on to serve a tour with the CIA in Korea. The Joint Advisory Commission Korea (JACK) was formed by April 1951 by combining the operations of the CIA's Office of Policy Coordination (OPC) with its Office of Special Operations (OSO), having Singlaub acting as Deputy Commander. While Western Enterprises and the Third Force operations were taking place by involving the Nationalists and Taiwan down south, JACK restricted its activities to the islands and mainland off the east side of North Korea. Special Mission Groups (SMG), operating from the nearby islands of Yong-do and Kadok-do, were tasked to destroy mainland North Korean railway infrastructure, bridges and roads along with the occasional odd job that may arise. JACK actually produced mixed results during its two years of operations. Singlaub, however, was more lauditory, "the very presence of guerrilla units behind the lines, regardless of how long they lasted, disrupted their lines of communications and harassed the North Korean military." [71]

One individual joining an SMG was Sgt. Thomas Fosmire, borrowed from Recon Company of the Army's 82nd Airborne Division. Fosmire recalled that fighters trained at the CIA facility on Saipan joined up with guerrillas he assisted in training on Kadok-do. A fishing trawler would be fitted to the hilt with armor-shielded light machine guns on either side and a heavy .50 caliber installed back of the wheelhouse. Powerful communication antennas were secretly hidden within the masts. The trawler was also made to transport up to 40 "Tiger Killers" guerrillas for operations ashore. To the North Koreans, the SMG fishing trawler had the appearance of a typical merchant boat like many others in Wonsan Bay. Fosmire and his compatriots ply the South Korean boat crew with cigarettes and liquor, which supplemented their typical compensation. Captain Kingston, who commanded one of the SMG's, was always certain to ensure there was adequate naval fire support for his coastal operations. [71]

> Kingston was briefing Commander Everett Glenn, skipper of the destroyer USS Moore, one day when Glenn commented:
>
> "You know, Captain, I always wanted to knock out a train."
>
> "Hell Sir, we'll get you a train!" Kingston proudly told him. [71]

Kingston provided Commander Glenn with a set of coordinates and then went ashore with some guerrillas taking along his ship-to-shore radio. They laid in wait near the exit to one of the railroad tunnels North Korea often used coming down the coast. Locomotives would often run without lights but when exiting the tunnel, you could still see the small flash from the steam engine's firebox. They waited around literally for hours until one finally came. On the moonless night, it was somewhat hard to see but Kingston and his men could definitely hear it. Then, as it was about to emerge from the tunnel...

"NOW!" Kingston quickly radioed to the USS Moore. Commander Glenn's destroyer opened up full bore with blasts of its twin 5-inch guns. "BOOM! BOOM!" [71]

Direct hits took out the enemy locomotive, derailing most of the train cars. Kingston later commented on how thrilled Commander Glenn was: "I thought the skipper was going to give me his ship." This may well have been the first time in the history of warfare that a Navy ship had taken out a moving train.

Newly assigned to JACK in 1953, Tony Poe made the acquaintance of Tom Fosmire, beginning a long-term friendship of closely working together on CIA projects. Fosmire and Poe would travel to Saipan to instruct the Chen-do Gyo with six weeks of paramilitary training. Saipan, wrought from the Japanese in 1944, now housed a Naval Training Facility at the north end of the island. The facility was also cover for secret CIA training of Nationalists, South Korean forces, and now the Chen-do Gyo. The latter weren't guerrillas but rather practitioners of a religion uniquely blending Buddhism with Catholic theology. Importantly, they absolutely hated the communists who had been persecuting them. Back to the mainland for advanced training, the militant religious group soon learned about the impending ceasefire, angry they hadn't yet gotten their pound of flesh. After one night of drinking, they almost took out their frustrations on Fosmire, their trainer. The ceasefire was formalized with the Korean Armistice being signed July 1953, effectively terminating guerrilla training and also the Joint Advisory Commission Korea (JACK). [19, 71]

Sgt. Fosmire was awarded the Bronze Star before returning stateside to an Army post but he later signed up on a permanent basis with the CIA and be transferred to Bangkok. Poe was also reassigned to Bangkok Station during the intervening years to work for Sea Supply Corporation, yet another CIA front organization. It was in Bangkok that Tony Poe met another CIA novice named Bill Lair.

# Taking Tibet

In January 1950, the communist party pronounced on radio its intent to "liberate" Taiwan, Hainan, and Tibet. While the island of Hainan was relatively easy, Taiwan, with its wider straits, staunch defenses and American support needed to be delayed to a more propitious time. Tibet wasn't easy either; with its high altitude, vast distances and lack of roads or airfields, it presented its own set of problems. Problems which Mao felt were surmountable. Furthermore, his liberation army had already absorbed the eastern portions of Amdo and Kham, and now it was time for the rest. [41, 44]

Mao, during the month of October 1950, directed his attention towards Tibet despite soon to be preoccupied with entering the Korean conflict. With the 18th Army of 20,000 under control of General Zhang Guihua, he easily defeated the ill-equipped Tibetan force of 8,500. Twenty engagements was all it took, ending with the battle for the town of Chamdo and its garrison. With the defeat, also came the surrender of the entire Kham region as well. Any further expansion into central Tibet required emplacement of better roadways and transportation infrastructure... and, of course, support of the young Dalai Lama. [41]

The US position respected Nationalist sovereignty over Tibet until Chiang Kai-shek was headed for defeat and the Communists threatened to take over. The Tibetan cabinet, during that time, asked for US assistance for Tibet to obtain membership in the United Nations. However, the US Secretary of State delayed and equivocated when it came time for taking appropriate action.

## Part One (1947-1954)

Tibet's supreme ruler was only 15 years old and while educated and well versed in religious scripture, he was a novice at diplomacy. Senior Tibetan officials tried to fill the void by again petitioning the United Nations to take up the case against the Chinese aggression. The world body was now absorbed with events in Korea and paid scant attention. By May 1951, in an attempt to appease Mao, Tibetan delegations were sent to Beijing where presumably under pressure, a 17 Point Agreement was signed, thus delineating procedures governing China's takeover of Tibet. Tibetan delegates were not authorized by the Dalai Lama to make decisions which bound Tibet but they signed documents, nonetheless. [41, 44]

Talks then proceeded in Kalimpong, India between Tibet and the US concerning asylum for the Dalai Lama in the US and conditions for acquiring limited military assistance. US Vice Counsel Nicholas Thacher specifically recalled:

> "I set about explaining the U.S. offer to grant asylum and material assistance. Very quickly, I was struck by the lack of realism displayed by Lhasa's envoys. There was a sense of the absurd.... they were talking wistfully in terms of America providing them with tanks and aircraft."

> "I tried my best to downplay their expectations," Thacher said.

Promises and expectations later became a recurring thorn in US and Tibetan relations. Provision of any military aid at this time required India's assent, in part due to transit necessary across Indian borders and also so as to not disrupt India's desire for cordial relations with China. The Tibetan government debated and formally adopted the 17 Point Agreement that September and Tibet would become a part of China. By mid 1952, China was actively engaged in developing a modern logistical network throughout key parts of Tibet, hiring Tibetan workers which also benefitted the local aristocracy who profited from the influx of Chinese. During this interlude, the American stance towards Tibet was one of non-involvement although it still needed to be kept abreast on what was happening in the region. Little did the US appreciate that the infrastructure buildout was actually meant to solidify China's hold on the immense new province. [41, 44]

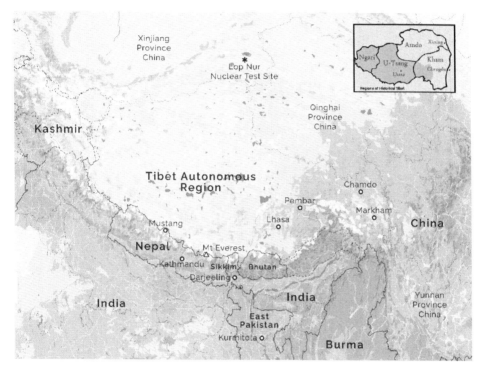

Tibet (1950s)

# Secrets of Marpi Point

Saipan is a small, hilly subtropical isle, born from volcanic disruption which had been under Japanese mandate since 1920. The island and its sister, Tinian, were the scenes of some of the bloodiest fighting during America's island-hopping quest during the Pacific War. It was a relentless drive to get ever closer to mainland Japan, within striking range for the Army Air Force's B-29 bombers. The battle and loss of Saipan resulted in the death of 24,000 Japanese, including a multitude of suicides: not to mention the resignation of Prime Minister Hideki Tojo. At the very northern end of Saipan sits Marpi Point and nearby cliffs appropriately named Banzai and Suicide where many civilians and Japanese soldiers alike jumped to their deaths. In one day alone, up to seven hundred jumped to their deaths, a tragedy which would be later repeated during the battle for Okinawa. Japanese propaganda alleged that Americans were brutal with prisoners, including mutilation of their war dead. The latter practice, while not being untrue, belies several massacres of Chamorro civilians the Japanese committed on nearby Guam. Tony Poe was known to have Chamorro ethnicity from his mother's side of the family. [27]

When the fighting ended in August 1944, Naval Construction Battalions, better known as Seabees, got to work repairing and enlarging airstrips, harbors and improving living areas. This included Marpi Point, where the Naval Tactical Training Unit (NTTU) in 1950 was located, the cover for secret CIA training. The entire north area was strictly secured and was also referred to as NAS Tanapag. In the area earlier known as Army Hill, a camp including administrative buildings, snack bar, post office, theater, and housing were built as well as a private airstrip.

---

Training there was performed in support of CIA missions throughout Far East Asia and likely an interrogation center similar to agency black sites found fifty years later. [90] While one of many secret areas, Saipan Training Station was easily secured, well equipped and probably the world's most remote facility from which to conduct covert training operations. Importantly, it was well distanced from intruding eyes of the media, Congress and the public.... or so it was thought. [41]

While Saipan was still under Japanese control, a plane crash landed in Garapan Harbor, about eight miles south of Marpi. The plane was a twin engine Lockheed Electra. Joaquina Cabrera, a young local launderer at the time, remembered seeing a white woman with short, cropped hair and wearing pants, taken under Japanese guard to a small building. Joaquina was handed the woman's leather jacket and instructed to wash her clothes....

> "She seemed like a sweet, gentle lady but she looked thin and very tired. She also didn't speak our language," Joaquina recalls.
>
> "Every day the Japanese would come to talk to her. She never smiled at them but she did smile to me. I think the Japanese police sometimes hurt her. She had many bruises and one time her arm appeared injured"
>
> "Then one day she was gone," a note of sadness entering her voice. "The police said that she had died of a disease." [27]

The year had been 1937 and Amelia Earhart, along with Fred Noonan, her navigator, were searching for Howland Island on their trip around the world. Japan was already chafing at perceived American breaching of their Pacific "barrier" of islands due to the success of Pan Am Airways establishing an ocean crossing two years earlier. Shortly after their capture, Noonan got separated from Amelia and was never heard from again. Some island witnesses remember attending a funeral cremation for a white woman, whom they didn't know.

## Part One (1947-1954)

Others, including Army personnel following the US takeover in 1944, recall seeing a Lockheed Electra, Model 10E, parked inside a Japanese hangar at Aslito Field. Shortly afterwards, the plane was destroyed by the American military and the whole matter kept a tight secret.

Fred Goerner, author of The Search for Amelia Earhart, came to Saipan in 1960 to speak with people and conduct a thorough investigation for his book. Coincidentally, the Saipan Training Station at Marpi Point was said to be shut down not long afterwards in 1962, likely out of concern his work would bring prying eyes. [27] Nature has largely reclaimed what remains of the old facilities but Radio Free Asia is said to still be broadcasting programs and messages into China, Vietnam and North Korea.... from somewhere at Marpi Point. [90]

Smaller Tinian Island, located about 14 miles south of Saipan was, as many know, the launch site for the B-29 Superfortress bombers delivering their atomic payload in August 1945. Further south was the island of Rota which was never invaded but did have a garrison of about thousand Japanese soldiers. When it was found that a radio transmitting from the island was warning Japan about the B-29s heading north, US bombers quickly silenced it. All islands are 75 miles or more north of Andersen AFB in Guam, which is still used on a rotational basis by the US Strategic Air Command. Tinian is presently being developed as an alternate airfield to Andersen should a major war ever break out with China. [90]

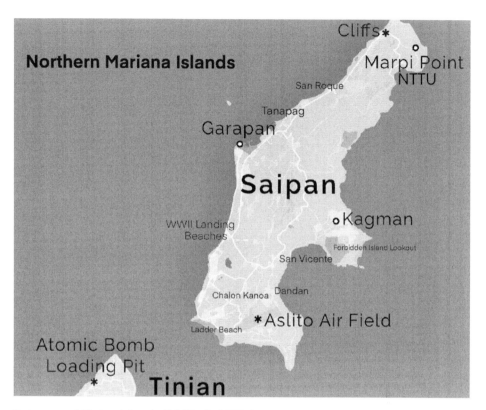

Saipan and Tinian Islands (1940s & 1950s)

# PART TWO (1954-1959)

# The City of Angels

"In agency training, we had been taught that every captured agent could be made to talk, and that they would talk eventually. What counted was how long the agent could delay before exchanging the cover story for the truth. Every fact held back, every day of stalling, would give the agency time to take measures or protect the lives of others. On the sixteenth night, I admitted I was a CIA agent, ... the confession was almost a relief." [6]

- John T. Downey (prison -year 2)

SEA Supply Corporation was a CIA front company set up by Paul Helliwell as a shipping concern with a mission similar to what Western Enterprises, Inc. did for the Nationalists in Taiwan. It was incorporated in Miami, with Bangkok offices first set up in September 1950. Also created in 1950 by William Pauley, a former Pan Am executive, was Civil Air Transport (CAT) based out of Taiwan to provide airlift support almost anywhere. Amongst their other duties, both organizations provided covert support for Kuomintang troops which, became stuck in Burma when most of Chiang's forces escaped to Taiwan in 1949. Between the two, they would take surplus American weapons stored in Taiwan for airlift to Shan State in northern Burma. [36]

The plan was for the General LiMi's Eighth Army in Burma to fight its way back up through Yunnan Province in the hopes of taking back China. He also needed more weapons to fight off Burma's attempt to oust him from their country. Two attempts on China were made in 1951 and the third and final one in August 1952. All were repelled by the Communists, resulting in heavy Nationalist casualties. Several CIA advisors who had accompanied the first invasion attempt of Yunnan also ended up being killed. So, about the time President Truman shut off the money spigot to LiMi's forces, the general focused greater attention on his expanding opium business.

Under the CIA code name, "Operation Paper" or Project LiMi as some would call it, Civil Air Transport flew their unmarked C-46's to Mong Hsat in Burma, returning back through Chiang Mai, Thailand. President Truman approved the plan, thinking that LiMi would cause Mao to divert some of his forces away from the Korean theater. CIA Director Walter B. Smith firmly believed the plan had little hope for success but the President overruled him. The arms for LiMi, as well as for training Thai Security forces, were taken from WWII stocks held on Okinawa. Initially, planes flew to Chiang Mai on the border and then the weapons were taken overland to LiMi's camp. At some point, deliveries were simplified and planes, instead of flying back empty, were said to be loaded up with opium on the return trip for later transport to Bangkok and distribution worldwide. Chief facilitator of drugs transiting Thailand was General Phao Sriyanond, acting head of the National Thai police force. [65]

The CIA and Thai government became worried when Mao's forces invaded both Korea and Tibet the same time in late 1950, having routed the Kuomintang just the year before. During the late 1940s, communist Chinese radio was sending propaganda broadcasts into Thailand as well. The troubling unanswered question was, "Is Southeast Asia next? Thailand?" In that atmosphere, the agency sent newly minted agent Bill Lair to Bangkok on his first assignment. He reported in to SEA Supply, Corp., initially located in a nondescript Thai house on Pra Athit Road and having only a few employees. Bangkok, in 1951, was an alluring Asian city about a tenth of the size today, with maybe more canals than streets. Locally it was known as Krung Thep, "the great city of angels where the immortal divinity dwells." Getting around was usually by streetcar, a smattering of automobiles but more often by non-motorized "sam-law", an oversized tricycle seating a couple passengers. Bangkok CIA station's attempt to get more information regarding China's intent was frustrating and also getting costly. Their primary means of doing so was by attempting to read the large volume of mail sent between China and Bangkok's Chinese community, necessitating a sizable crew of translators. Given the generalized fear of invasion, the Thai Post Office became unsurprisingly compliant. [36]

SEA Supply's instructions were for Lair, and a certain police captain, to set up a paramilitary camp for training officers to guard Thailand's extensive borders against communist intrusion. He also needed General Phao's blessing to do so which, surprisingly, was more easily obtained than anticipated. Maybe, the general saw for himself an opportunity to obtain a private army, trained and paid for by the American government. Lair began setting up a paramilitary program with a curriculum mixing US Army techniques with what he learned from his CIA training. Jump training was also added on for good measure. Those initially trained would go on to become course instructors themselves. They called themselves Police Aerial Reinforcement Unit or PARU but were still a part of the Border Patrol Police. The program made a name for themselves and later added courses in medical technology and communications, including development of a "lingua franca" based on a phonetic version of Thai language. This allowed the CIA to also listen in on important radio traffic. Importantly, with the camp relocated from Lopburi to Hua Hin, summer residence of the monarchy, King Bhumibol, began to take an active interest in the PARU program. [51]

By late 1953, the Border Patrol Police itself became well established with 94 platoons deployed along Thailand's borders. As the communist infiltration threat diminished, Lair's core PARU were transformed into a cross-border commando unit necessitating guerrilla and anti-insurgency training. This was the time Tony Poe, following the Korean Armistice, reported to Walter Kuzmak at SEA Supply ostensibly to provide needed supplemental instruction, as did his buddy Tom Fosmire. American weapons such as M1 rifles, carbines, mortars, bazookas and grenade launchers were provided as part of the training. During a September 1957 coup, General Phao was forced into exile while a reconstituted PARU was brought under the control of the Thai army and took on a major role in Laos.

## Part Two (1954-1959)

Tony Poe, Tom Fosmire and Bill Lair are a study of contrasts: Lair graduated from Texas A & M in June 1950, the same time that Poe obtained his degree from San Jose State. Both men made use of the G.I. Bill after putting in their military service in different theaters during World War II. Lair landed on Omaha Beach as a member of an Army mortar platoon, fighting his way across France before ending up facing the Russians across the Elbe. While his buddies celebrated conclusion of the war with wine and womanizing, young Bill took to reading books and retracing Hemingway's steps throughout France. Even at A & M, Lair wasn't your typical party animal, nor did he mention in his memoirs any old flames or school buddies. He got through his four years as an Aggie, culminating with a degree in geology. Lair is tall, quiet, modest yet self assured. Tony Poe, by comparison, with his booming voice was brash, stocky, a heavy drinker yet often inspiring as a leader. The Thai hierarchy easily took to Lair with his respectful and self-effacing manner. As to Tom Fosmire, he was the efficient "everyman" lying somewhere between the extremes of the other two men. When it came to Poe, you either loved or hated him... there was little or no middle road. The CIA had a name for the paramilitary guys best epitomized by Poe: they called them "Knuckle draggers."

Paul Helliwell, an OSS Colonel during World War II, was considered a master at setting up agency cover organizations. In many cases, the outfits actually conducted legitimate business while also performing covert work for the CIA. A prime example would be Civil Air Transport (CAT) which was actually started by Claire Chennault in 1946. It was pressed into service on behalf of Chiang Kai-shek's forces during the Chinese Civil War and assisted with their evacuation to Taiwan in 1949. The airline flew regular passenger routes and also C-46s and C-47s for the agency initially by pilots from Chennault's Flying Tigers. CAT flew those weekly airlifts into and out of Burma, being sure of course, to use only their unmarked planes. It was a CAT C-47, carrying Downey and Fecteau, that was shot down over Manchuria in November 1952. [36]

Helliwell may or may not have had some hand in Civil Air Transport's creation but he certainly did with SEA Supply. His expertise was derived from experience of being a businessman, lawyer as well as a banker. The CIA required small banks and businesses to skirt applicable banking laws while operating an under-the-radar profile. According to author Joseph Trento, Helliwell is "known to have pioneered the art of illegally financing intelligence activity to avoid bureaucratic accountability." That meant quietly pushing around money to where and when the agency needed it most. [36]

The banks which Helliwell set up to funnel, launder and distribute money were named Mercantile Bank & Trust and the Castle Bank & Trust. By 1960, they were chartered in the Bahamas as off-shore banks with Helliwell now keeping a SEA Supply office in Miami to service clients including the CIA, organized crime and endeavors to depose Castro. As a result of IRS Operation Tradewinds, many of the agency's financial dealings were exposed, leading to dissolution of the Helliwell banks. Bernard Houghton, Mike Hand and Frank Nugen, in 1973, took up the mantle of funneling CIA money by establishing Nguyen Hand Bank in Australia. Operations were similar to Helliwell's and lessons learned by the Helliwell experience were applied but at that time was all on a much grander scale, with branches established throughout the world. [36]

# Tumultuous Times

"In a Chinese prison, a man's five senses do not atrophy because they are deprived of stimulus. Instead, they are always hungry and therefore always acute. Their relative importance, though, may be reordered. The ears begin to tell more than the eyes; smell becomes more sensuous than touch..." [6]

John T. Downey (prison -year 3)

Everyday life in mid-1950s America could be quite enjoyable, somewhat insulated and yet also promising. The Korean War was now over, Senator Joe McCarthy's Communist witch hunt approached a decline after Edward R. Murrow's broadcast and "Earth Angel" by the Penguins hit the top spot on the R & B charts. Best movie in 1954 was "White Christmas" starring Bing Crosby and Danny Kaye. A top selling book, however, was "Lord of the Flies" a reminder that not all was good in the world. As a best seller, it explored issues of morality in governance, living in harmony, the dangers of groupthink and respect for the individual. Themes that were being played out not on a fictional island, but also in real life.

The Korean Conflict was wrapping up. Operation Glory took place in the second half of 1954, following a complicated prisoner swap the year before. This time it involved exchange of deceased soldiers between belligerent countries of the Korean War. A total 13,528 dead Chinese and North Korean soldiers were exchanged for 4,167 US military dead. Of the American deaths, there were 416 unidentified who were buried as unknown soldiers in the National Memorial Cemetery of the Pacific in Hawaii, commonly referred to as "The Punchbowl," In total, the US suffered 33,651 battle deaths during the war. The Korean War would go down as the deadliest Cold War era conflict culminating in deaths of over 3 million people, the majority being civilians. The percentage of civilian deaths was said, by some historians, to be higher than in Vietnam or even World War II. Seeing the successful Communist takeover of Vietnam twenty years later, Kim Il-sung, in mid-1975 asked Mao again for military support to reunite Korea. This time Mao wisely refused. [27]

While tensions may have eased on the peninsula, it was revving up in the Taiwan Straits. The First Taiwan Straits Crisis is also known as the Quemoy-Matsu Crisis. Chiang's Nationalist army had 58,000 troops stationed on Quemoy and another 15,000 on Matsu, islands sitting just a few miles off the Chinese mainland. By 1954, the CIA operations, Third Force and Western Enterprises, had run their respective course. US defense aid continued to be provided via the Military Assistance Advisory Group (MAAG) on Taiwan and of course, the Seventh Fleet was still actively patrolling the Taiwan Strait. Units of the Peoples Liberation Army now relieved of fighting on the Korea peninsula, were sent south with China's Zhou Enlai proclaiming in August that Taiwan "must be liberated as an exercise of China's sovereignty." The PLA then unleashed a heavy artillery barrage on Quemoy, during which time American advisors Lieutenant Colonels Lynn and Medendorp were killed. Matsu and Dachen island were also shelled. Taiwan and nearby Pescadores islands located 30 miles away were brought into a mutual defense agreement between the US and Taiwan. Dachen was reluctantly evacuated, with the Seventh Fleet removing the 14,300 civilians and 10,000 troops to Taiwan by early 1955. Around the same time that Dachen was evacuated, the National Security Council reversed its earlier position and agreed to extend the defense agreement to also cover Quemoy and Matsu. [73, 74]

During the height of the crisis, the Joint Chiefs of Staff recommended the use of nuclear weapons, presumably not the tactical kind, against the Chinese mainland. President Eisenhower resisted doing so and decided against getting

## Part Two (1954-1959)

American troops involved. It's felt that China backed down due to US threats to use nuclear bombs on the mainland and the Soviet Union's reluctance to retaliate on behalf of China. Some historians believe this all was Mao's pretext to initiate his own nuclear program. The following year, the Chinese Politburo gave him the authority to pursue nuclear weapons research. By 1964, they were doing testing and in 1967, the first Chinese hydrogen bomb was detonated. [74]

Mao's original idea was to consider the Battle of Chamdo as laying the foundation for the liberation of Tibet. Essentially, the Tibetan "liberation" or revolution was considered to be an extension of the Chinese Revolution... the struggle between the classes. The classes meaning, of course, feudal landowners and the peasantry. However, Mao cautioned his propaganda machine against using words that could be considered offensive to Tibetan ruling party. General Zhang, commanding the Chinese forces, was ordered to use a more tolerant policy toward the Tibetan lamas and aristocrats in power. The Communists, Mao felt, needed them to first create a "bridge" to reach the common people. This approach was most uncharacteristic of Mao who typically believed in results quickly achieved by using military might. Mao's objective with Tibet was to take over the region quickly, due to perceived outside threats, then to reform Tibet's feudal system which took much longer. There was some internal debate on whether to use the Panchen Lama or the Dalai Lama. The Dalai Lama ultimately had higher authority but he was still relatively young. The Panchen Lama laid his claim by exhibiting twenty years of patriotic service and loyalty. There was also the matter of Tibetans 'deep spirituality involving Lamaism which Mao felt needed to be dealt with carefully. While the go-slow process of reformation was taking place, the roads and airfields continued to be constructed at a consistent pace. [41, 44]

In 1954, both the Panchen Lama and the Dalai Lama were invited to Beijing to attend the National People's Congress. The hosting of the two Tibetan leaders and their respective delegations took place over a period of several months. After 1955, the policy of waiting and going slow in Tibet changed course. The time for reform began and so did clashes in two autonomous Tibetan prefectures of Sichuan Province. [41, 44]

In Vietnam, the Battle of Dien Bien Phu, began in March 1954 and almost two months later, forever ended French colonial involvement in Vietnam. The French originally came to Indochina back in 1884 and after World War II, wanted to reestablish its rule again in 1946. Ho Chi Minh and his Viet Minh soldiers felt otherwise and began resisting using guerrilla warfare. When China and the Soviet Union stepped in with equipment and material support, the conflict took on more conventional military aspects. Support that included captured American heavy artillery and anti-aircraft guns. In the village of Dien Bien Phu, situated only nine miles from the Laos border, the Viet Minh had amassed 49,000 troops, comprising of 5 divisions and commanded by General Vo Nguyen Giap. The Viet Minh held all the nearby high ground easily raining down artillery shells upon 9,000 French soldiers hunkered below. French General Henri Navarre had deluded himself into thinking there was but one Vietnamese division; notwithstanding intel from his own Air Force, he was greatly underestimating the extent of enemy forces. [47, 74]

The United States was picking up much of the French costs during the conflict, not so much for want of French colonialism but as a bulwark against the spread of communism. The US approved assistance to France in May 1950, following their request four months earlier. To protect their investment, a Military Advisor Assistance Group was established that fall but the French were resistant to accepting US military advice until 1953 when it was much too late. China had already recognized the Ho Chi Minh government in January 1950, including moving its troops up to the Indochina border. China apparently had been keeping an eye on Southeast Asia, and Vietnam in particular, even before tensions broke out on the Korean Peninsula. By 1954, United States had already spent $1 billion and was now picking up 80% of France's military costs in Vietnam. [81]

Ho Chi Minh is known to have written President Truman several times, including a letter in January 1946 following the President's address to the United Nations. The address mentioned every nation's right of self-determination based on principles laid down in the Atlantic Charter of 1941. Ho was asking for US help to stop recolonization of Vietnam by France. Unfortunately, Ho Chi Minh

Part Two (1954-1959)

mentioned reconstruction help was needed from both China and the US. While admiring the principles of America's founding fathers, Ho had been a known communist going back to the 1920s. He never received a reply from President Truman. [74, 81]

Things were looking bad for Navarre's redoubt at Dien Bien Phu; however, the US was reluctant to provide overt support to the beleaguered French. They did dedicate 24 Civil Air Transport (CAT) pilots flying C-119s painted over with French Air Force markings for resupply operations. CIA Director Allen Dulles appealed to other countries to participate... after Britain had firmly declined to get involved.

CIA Director, Allen Dulles, was reported to have offered atomic bombs to the French in April. Additionally, Joint Chief of Staff Chairman Admiral Arthur Radford was known to have discussed the possibility of supplying the French with smaller, tactical nuclear weapons. While that didn't happen, Admiral Radford did provide the French with two squadrons B-26 Invader bombers with crews operated under the direction of Allen Dulles. In France, the general public was shocked that the Viet Minh, a guerrilla army, was on the verge of defeating a major European power. But this was no longer the indigent guerrilla force that it once was. [74]

The Eisenhower administration was in continuous debate as to whether they should intervene in the Indochina conflict and, if doing so, how it would be done. Voices were strong on both sides of the aisle with unpleasant memories still lingering from the Korean War advocating against any intervention.

The US National Security Council met on April 6, 1954, and the major topic of discussion, understandably, was the worsening situation at Dien Bien Phu. There was concern that there was "very grave danger" China would enter the conflict if the US overtly doing so caused a defeat of the Viet Minh. There was some question whether additional Chinese advisors or maybe even a Chinese general was on the ground but no confirmation was given that was so. Additionally, there was no verification that Chinese soldiers were manning anti-aircraft guns speculating why their fire had been so accurate. Quite apparent from this

Security Council meeting was the fear of being dragged into another war with China. President Eisenhower, near the end of the conference, commented on the slim chance of getting Congress to approve intervention on behalf of the French. [74]

> "There is no possibility whatsoever of US unilateral intervention in Indochina, and we had better face that fact. At the very least, we would have to be invited in by Vietnam"

American soldiers would not be entering the fight in Vietnam.... at least not in 1954.

A major 1954 Conference in Geneva ended in July with the decision to break up French Indochina into the Kingdoms of Cambodia, Laos and to partition North from South Vietnam. The plan was for Vietnam to hold an election in two years to unite the country but that never happened. The conference also dealt with lingering Korea issues in an attempt to hold elections, possibly unifying the country. That was not accomplished as well. In the spring of 1955, the Bandung Conference was held In Indonesia. Twenty-nine countries attended to what would later become the Non-Aligned Movement, a movement resistant to growing Communist/West polarization that was occurring during the Cold War. It would also take an anti-colonialist position. [74, 81]

The US government did not send an official to the Bandung Conference as they feared taking a stance might alienate their European colonialist allies. China, however, did send Zhou Enlai, their Premier which a CIA team attempted to assassinate. The plan involved Captain William Corson, a Marine assigned to the US Consulate in Hong Kong. As Corson later relates....

> "The plan was to place a bowl of rice, laced with a slow-acting toxin, in front of where Zhou Enlai was seated for a group meal. He would become ill but wouldn't die until he had actually returned back to China"

"After I got the team together, we practiced the plan over and over in Macau and also in Jakarta. We even had a Chinese guy on Zhou's security detail secretly working for us". Two of the team members would be dressed as waiters.

"Zhou took his seat and the waiters placed the correct bowl in front of him. Right at that moment my communications man and the driver ran in frantically waving the signal to... ABORT ! , ABORT ! As also per the plan, the waiters very quickly took away the tainted rice bowl. But now but the Indonesian security people saw what was happening and the drew their guns" [40]

"Shots rang out. Two of my men were shot trying to get away. I was hit in the side."

Corson, while recovering in Hong Kong was debriefed on the aborted attempt by Senator Prescott Bush. Bush was President Eisenhower's personal advisor on the most secret covert operations, that sometimes even the CIA wasn't fully aware of. Senator Bush was most curious about potential blowback which could possibly implicate the White House. Corson seemed to give Bush enough assurance that there shouldn't be any problems. The father of the 41st US President would leave Hong Kong fully satisfied. [40]

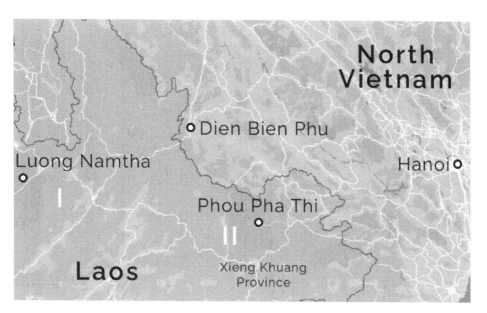

Dien Bien Phu, Vietnam (1950s)

# The Road to Leadville

In early spring 1956, thirty-year-old Ella Burnett was driving up from Gilman, Colorado to Leadville's St. Francis hospital to check on one of her patients who had been transferred there. She was raised in nearby Red Cliff and since 1947, had been the only nurse at the seven-bed Gilman Hospital primarily in charge of delivering babies. While turning the dial on her car radio to bring in KBRR in Leadville..... she thinks to herself, "Yea, Brrr is right,", with snow blanketing the ground and her car heater fighting a losing battle against the cold. Suddenly, while twisting the knob back and forth, an old favorite comes on, "I've Got a Gal in Kalamazoo" by the Glenn Miller Band. Ella quickly finds herself humming right along with it [81, 79]

Camp Hale soon appears in view on the left side and Ella's mind drifts back to fond memories she had while attending Saturday night dances there. Each town had a bevy of young ladies who were bussed to camp to attend various USO activities. The dances were a much-anticipated event and at one point, the seventeen-year-old beauty was even voted Miss Red Cliff. *"Oh, what fun that was,"* she thought. Ella recalled the young soldiers, some shy and others more bold but all respectful and handsome in their uniforms. With a tinge of melancholy Ella wondered if the ones she had danced with made it safely back from the war. As peace descended upon the ugliness of war, were they able to find love, happiness, maybe even start families of their own. The reminiscing soon evaporated as she focused on the patient she was about to see.

Camp Hale was built in 1942 to house and train the 10th Mountain Division and associated units for World War II. It became a self-contained city with mess halls, theaters, a field house, stables for pack mules and barracks for up to 10,000 soldiers training for winter warfare, including skiing, mountaineering and acquiring alpine survival skills. The valley previously was called Eagle Park with the Eagle River meandering through the middle and ponds to make ice blocks in the winter. To accommodate the many camp structures and roads needed, the river was straightened out and nearby Highway 24 rerouted further away. Nearby Leadville ballooned in size once the soldiers were permitted to visit town but shrank again after the war. Almost a thousand soldiers who had trained at Camp Hale perished while fighting in the rugged mountains of Italy. [81]

Ella is a member of the demographic cohort known as the "Greatest Generation", the grouping whose men fought and women served during World War II bringing an end to tyrannical rulers and fascist ideology. Ella, now 96 years old, is well known and revered today in these parts as the consummate caregiver. In fact, many would owe their very start in life to Nurse Ella Burnett. [79]

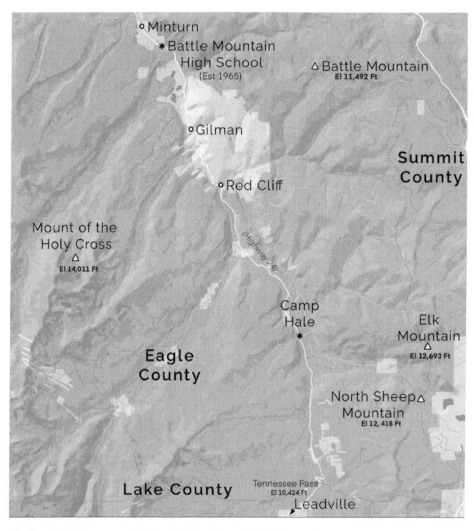

Upper Eagle County, Colorado (1950s & 1960s)

# The Superpower Program

"We can improve your conditions', he said, as a guard approached from somewhere and began to unlock my reviled shackles. The chains fell away and suddenly my legs were my own again. Without taking a step, I could feel their lightness; my whole body felt the freedom and the sigh of release." [6]

- John T. Downey (prison -year 4)

Following the Korean War in 1953, Mao Tse-Tung realized he couldn't rely on his massive army and human wave attacks to win battles. His objective was to focus on industrialization, more specifically on building up his arms industry with emphasis on sophisticated weaponry. He therefore began his goal to build up China into a military superpower within his lifetime. Early on, military spending took up a whopping 61% of the budget when compared with only 8.2 % for education and health care. He told his people that the military equipment from the Soviet Union was a gift but it wasn't: it was all being paid for dearly, as it came down to China selling their agriculture products for military equipment. What Mao was exporting was the basic nutrition essentials needed by his own people, such as grains, dairy and protein products. The impact fell almost entirely on the peasantry, already among the poorest in the world, who were left to starve when inevitable food shortages began to occur. Mao proclaimed:

"Having only tree leaves to eat? Well so be it.... we will need to educate the peasants simply to eat less!" [1]

## Part Two (1954-1959)

It was an attitude eerily reminiscent of his siege of Changchun five years earlier. This was Mao's Superpower Program which existed through the 1950s, well before the Great Leap Forward in 1958. The thing Mao genuinely wanted from this program, what he really coveted most... was the technology to build an atomic bomb. A closely guarded secret that Stalin, and later Khrushchev, were most reluctant to reveal. [1]

Towards the end of China's first National People's Congress, Mao began to show his other true colors. He had been self-disciplining long enough and said what had been burning in his mind. Taking the young Dalai Lama aside for some old sage wisdom, he told him that religious faith was like a poison. To the Dalai Lama's ears, this was tantamount to utmost blasphemy. It became perfectly clear now where he and Tibet stood with respect to Chairman Mao and the Chinese.

As the Dalai Lama headed back to Tibet in early 1955, following the Beijing conference, he made note that the road from Kham to Lhasa was now completed, as was a second road from Amdo to the capital. The latter road of three possible routes became the preferred one used by the Chinese to resupply their troops in Tibet. The Chinese had introduced atheist teaching in Tibetan schools and begun implementation of a harsh agrarian collectivization program. This quickly sparked a wave of violence in eastern Tibet, beginning with the nomads in the Golok region of Amdo followed by more organized resistance in the eastern Kham.

The Khampas assembled twenty-three clan leaders and attacked a string of isolated Chinese enclaves. They were fierce warriors in their own right and said to be feared by most Chinese soldiers. Averaging almost 6 foot in height, Khampas were renowned for their superior horsemanship and marksmanship. Equestrian skills, however, were no match when the communists responded by sending in several Tupelev-4 bombers leading to the deaths of thousands. The air campaign also allowed the Chinese to send in additional troops to retake their garrisons, destroying the large monastery at Lithang in the process. [41, 44]

The Tibetan change from passive resistance to armed warfare had caught the United States completely off guard. Washington's previous stance of non-commitment now required a more coherent and active policy. The Far East Division at CIA headquarters still had no officer assigned solely to Tibetan affairs but that would soon change. The Khampas, desperate for assistance, began seeking help from the Kuomintang who also had no great love for the communists. Gyalo Thondrup, older secular brother to the Dalai Lama, decided to actively intervene, advising the Khampas to avoid of the Nationalists. Chiang's government, while hating the Communists, are nonetheless Chinese and also had a claim to Tibet. "Be wary of their aims," he said. Gyalo advised them of a better source from which to seek assistance from would be the Americans. [41, 44]

Out of an initial group of twenty-seven Khampa candidates, six were selected for additional training by the CIA. Off they flew under great secrecy, not to Guam as some had expected but to Saipan. The CIA training at Saipan Training Station was quite varied, having trained Chinese Nationalists, Koreans, Indonesians and even the Vietnamese to form their own version of the CIA. Concurrent instruction of various nationalities were accommodated due to the compartmentalization of each training sector.

Roger McCarthy, finished from his Western Enterprise days, first arrived on Saipan in 1956. In March the next year, he received a terse message simply stating, "Six Tibetans will be arriving for training." Upon arrival, the Tibetans presented their own unique set of problems. A year's worth of curriculum needed to be condensed into a space of 3 months, foremost emphasizing communications and reporting skills. As one agency trainer later said, "the recruits were to act as the CIA's eyes and ears when they're back in Tibet." Accordingly, it shaped the instruction syllabus and necessitated an understanding of the twenty-four-hour clock, and properly quantifying distances and numbers. Approximations and vague references were no longer acceptable. Also, classroom instruction was limited as the Tibetans often required pictorial or on-the-scene visualization to grasp a concept. Additionally, since their reading and writing skills were subpar, basic classes in Tibetan grammar were needed to enhance accuracy in their reporting. [41, 44]

Other courses in espionage, tradecraft, guerrilla warfare and use of the short-wave radio augmented the curriculum. The emphasis was on active reconnaissance rather than fighting. Ultimately, being Buddhists and mostly former monks, there was some concern whether the Tibetans would be hesitant on taking another person's life. The CIA quickly realized, however, they had no qualms about taking the life of a Chinese invader. A disconnect soon formed between what the agency wanted and Tibetan expectations of freeing their country. The recruits asked for heavy machine guns and artillery, weaponry which McCarthy had to tactfully deny or downplay in necessity. One Tibetan had even requested an atomic bomb to take back with them. [41]

# Where the Eagles Fly

By mid 1958, Desmond Fitzgerald took over the CIA's Far East Division, giving the green light to having training in a climate more similar to Tibet itself. That task fell to John Greaney who flew to Colorado first liaising with Fort Carson in Colorado Springs which retained administrative control over a training site near Leadville in the central Colorado mountains. After a personal visit to the completed training camp, General Richard Risden at Fort Carson fell over backwards, lending whatever support was needed to the secret enclave. Risden, himself, had earlier been Army Chief of the MAAG on Taiwan where he cultivated good relations with the CIA. [41, 44]

When John Greaney drove up to the 9,200-elevation former 10th Mountain Division camp in early fall, he saw much that impressed him. Despite residual evidence of where the 10th's WWII camp had been located, an attractive alpine mountain valley presented itself ringed by peaks jutting above the tree line. The area was sparsely populated and the air crisp and dry, a welcome respite from the humidity of places such as Saipan. The only problem was the facilities. Most of the former buildings were now gone, except for a few administrative structures within sight and proximity to Denver & Rio Grande tracks running the length of the valley. For needed secrecy, that was much too close to prying eyes. A more removed location for the camp would offer better concealment but required laying additional water and sewage pipes. That took some time, given the hardening ground in late season. Tom Fosmire was tasked with finding a temporary training site during this construction period. He ended up choosing a remote corner of Camp Peary, also known as "The Farm", where CIA recruits underwent boot camp. Fosmire then hustled off to Kurmitola, Pakistan to escort back the second batch of Tibetan trainees, this time ten in number. [41, 44]

As Fosmire took over the training, he was soon joined by several other agents. At one point, Ken Knaus, Chinese linguist and doctoral candidate, stopped in to lecture the Tibetans about the Chinese system and evils of communism. Of course, his students were already well aware of the latter. Tall, thin and bespectacled, Knaus represented the brainy side of the CIA. He was anxious to get out into the field but in later years took over as head of the Tibet Task Force after Roger McCarthy. Following Ken Knaus was Tony Poe, linking up once again with his old friend Tom Fosmire. Poe's job contrasted with Knaus' classroom teaching... he taught the necessary paramilitary skills, including guerrilla warfare, survival and weaponry. By spring 1959, the Tibetan Task Force had moved all its training to their new digs at Camp Hale. Right about the same time the Dalai Lama escaped, seeking asylum in India. [41, 44]

Unbeknownst to the people of Llasa, the Dalai Lama was well on his way out of the country when full-scale rioting in the city broke out. Popular discontent was joined by the Tibetan army to which the Chinese military responded in full force by shelling artillery rounds. In four days time, the rioting was brutally quelled. [41]

Not being heard from in a week, the world held its collective breath, wondering... "Where is the Dalai Lama? Was he captured?... IS HE EVEN ALIVE?" The first to find out was the CIA. A message was delivered by horseback to Althar, of the first group which had parachuted in, at his base camp in Lhuntse Dzong. From there, Althar radioed his contact on Okinawa that Tibet's god-king was now safe and sound. Along with the radio message, it included the request: "You must help us.... send weapons for 30,000 men by airplane." In short order, President Eisenhower himself was advised of the positive developments. Listening to his transistor radio, the Dalai Lama found out that Mao had unilaterally dissolved the Tibetan government upon learning of his escape. In response, the twenty-three-year-old Tibetan leader repudiated the Seventeen Point Agreement signed in 1951 and quickly reestablished his dissolved government. The Dalai Lama now also made a point of inserting the word "independence" into his speeches. [41, 44, 73]

The third batch of trainees was selected from a much larger pool of candidates. This time the contingent numbered twenty-three with three of them being translators. Taken by train from Dacca to Kurmitola, they boarded a bus having blacked out windows and were deposited at the rear door of an unmarked C-118 aircraft. Inside to greet them was none other than Tony Poe.

> "Americans were so big!" was the first impression of one of the interpreters looking at Tony Poe. "I was stunned by his height." [44]

After undergoing physical exams and aptitude tests on Okinawa, the group whittled down to twenty recruits. The CIA was making headway in increasing its Tibetan training program but the Chinese Army always seemed to be a step ahead. The Tibetans were prone to making mistakes by fighting in groups too large, planning needlessly complex operations and neglecting to use knowledge of the terrain to their advantage. They needed more than arms, they required training to effectively utilize small unit guerrilla warfare involving hit-and-run tactics. It's a similar problem which bedeviled the CIA working with indigenous fighters in Laos, almost a decade later. Of particular concern was the Communist army's ability now to keep supplies and troop reinforcements flowing due to the road network they'd built traversing the Tibet plateau. It was a similar situation to America's need years later to interdict the North Vietnamese flow of supplies coming down the Ho Chi Minh Trail. [41, 44]

The Amdo road was the chosen route favored by Chinese to supply their army in Tibet. Eisenhower considered using air strikes against the roadway to make logistics a costlier proposition for Mao. This was ruled out, however, in favor of Tibetan guerrilla squads parachuted in to slow down resupply efforts. Training became better defined... reconnaissance, supply interdiction, guerrilla-style harassment soon shaped the instructional curriculum and weapons used.

## Part Two (1954-1959)

After the C-118 landed, group three of the trainees boarded a covered bus at Peterson Field in Colorado Springs for their 170-mile bus trip up to Camp Hale. It was now May 1959 and stepping out into the cool pre-dawn air of Camp Hale, the change was immediately palpable. It was light enough to see snow-capped mountains as one interpreter would exclaim, "It looked and felt like we were home in Tibet!" Tony Poe, Tom Fosmire and six Khampas transferred from Camp Peary were there to meet the new arrivals. The Tibetan consensus was they absolutely loved their new training setting so much so that they called it "Dumra", which in their language means "The Garden." [42, 44]

Between September 1959 and January 1960, four separate groups of Camp Hale trainees were dropped into Tibet. They weren't just Khampas but now also Tibetan Muslims and Buddhist monks who had enough of Chinese tyranny. Dechen and Bhusang were among the latter groups and remember their training days as being concentrated and rigorous going six days a week with only Sunday afternoon off. On Sunday, relaxation, volleyball and maybe a keg of beer was the order of the day. Training was enhanced from what the first trainee group learned on Saipan. It included not only the usual radio communications and demolitions but also heavy weapons such as bazookas, mortars, machine guns and the recoilless rifle; bigger weapons which could still be easily airlifted into Tibet. CIA instructors frequently doubled up as cooks, bus drivers, and clothes cleaners and on their own time off they'd duck into nearby Leadville, for a brew and burger at the Sky City Bar. [41, 44]

Of course, being in Colorado's high country, winter warfare and survival skills could now be coached as well. Dechen said the instructors, themselves, were taught a thing or two by the Tibetans when it came to not leaving telltale tracks in the snow. They ditched the snowshoes and the lead person would attach rags and broken branches to their legs compressing a narrow path in the snow for others to follow. The serpentine path was almost impossible to spot. They also had no fear of heights, a fondness for blowing things up and a relentless enthusiasm punctuated by occasional bouts of humor. Bhusang recalls occasionally watching movies in the clubhouse such as "Viva Zapata!" starring Marlin Brando. The movie's theme resonated with many of them to the point one of the trainees made a Mexican sombrero which he often wore around the compound. They loved American movies, the culture and the modern-day conveniences. Both men were impressed when the President sent them his framed portrait with the message, "To my Tibetan Friends," signed Dwight Eisenhower. Tom Fosmire later remarked, "The Tibetans really moved you in their direction."

[42, 44]

Tony Poe also made his mark with the Tibetans. The man they referred to simply as "Mr. Tony" could be a little gruff but they respected him, nonetheless. One time, the US Army brought up four mules to Camp Hale to be retrained as pack mules. Poe, of all people, was put in charge of these stubborn beasts which bit and kicked him plus other Americans who attempted to train them. Whacking one on the hindquarters with his clipboard certainly did not endear them to Tony Poe. Bhusang recalled using a different tact of speaking softly to them for hours as if they were human beings. The patient approach worked as the mules quickly became domesticated and compliant again. [41, 44]

The final planned mission took place in March 1961 which was led by Yeshe Wangyal whose father had been leading a resistance cell but was recently killed. The plan was for Yeshe's group to parachute in near Markham, His hometown in eastern Tibet was also at the terminus of a major Chinese Army supply route that the CIA wanted disrupted. Before beginning the long trip from Colorado, Yeshe was allowed to select his own team, totaling seven. He chose his capable friend Bhusang, a thirty-two-year-old former doctor from Lhasa, as his deputy. Larger Air Force C-130s were now being used and Takhli Air Base in central Thailand was the last refueling stop before heading north into Tibet. Takhli would become the air base of choice for CIA operations instead of Kurmitola, East Pakistan, with Thai PARU soldiers packing pallets of weapons for airdrops as they had done for the Indonesian insurgents. During the Vietnam War, the base would also host a succession of US tactical fighter squadrons.

The flight over the "hump" — as the Himalayas were known to pilots — was uneventful in part because the means to safely airlift supplies and men had been perfected. All men landed safely, however, it was over 60 miles from the designated drop zone. The following week, the overland journey went without incident but now they had consumed almost all their food. In sight of Markham, Yeshe speaks with a nomad who informs him the locals knew about the C-130 flying over a week before and that the Chinese were now actively patrolling the area. They met the vestiges of Yeshe's father's group hiding in the forest: a sad, ragged and half-starved group including many women and children. Despite exhortations from Yeshe and Bhusang, the rebels were at the end of their rope and headed south towards India instead. They had their fill of five years of war with the Chinese. [41]

Apparently, their presence was tipped off to the Chinese who had closed in on Yeshe's group. Nine different running firefights ensued on the first day alone. They tried to escape by climbing up the mountain but the Chinese controlled the heights and other potential exits. Chinese soldiers had adapted to the methods and tactics used by Tibetan rebels.

> At daybreak of the final day, Bhusang took stock of their situation. "Squeezed between boulders, I could hear Yeshe's sister and two children weeping loudly. Looking around ,I saw two from our team huddled behind a rock outcropping and Yeshe and another behind a third.
>
> "The Chinese were edging closer and reduced their shooting to call for us to surrender. 'Eat Shit!!' we would yell back.
>
> "You invaded our country! What do mean surrender !?" The shooting ratcheted back up again. "It became intense, unreal... like in a dream," Bhusang later recalled.
>
> Now even more closer, the Chinese grabbed the wailing children. "I looked round to see that two of my comrades had taken their cyanide capsules which we

each carried as a last resort. They were motionless, likely dead.

"We all had a discussion the night before about committing suicide after each of us had fired our last shot. I quickly glanced around to see Yeshe motioning that he was about to take his, so I put a capsule in my mouth as well." [44]

Before Bhusang could bite down on his pill, a Chinese soldier slammed his rifle butt into the back of his neck and he was taken prisoner. Bhusang La spent the next eighteen years in a Chinese prison, finally being released in 1978. He was the only survivor from the Camp Hale team of seven. Shortly before his death at age 80, Bhusang reflected on his years of incarceration, saying:

"All those years I was treated like an animal. I've been tortured on and on and still I've been able to survive. Whenever the Chinese tortured me, I thought, *Such people exist in the world and we have done nothing to them.* I am proud I have been able to survive and to have done my bit when I was in my own country." [41]

Roger McCarthy, who in 1957 served as an instructor to the first group on Saipan, was now thirty-two years old. Impressing his superiors, he was known for his gregarious nature and having a soft spot for the Tibetan's plight. McCarthy took over the reins of Tibetan Task Force from Frank Holober in March 1959 and proved to be just as popular with the Tibetans. [41]

During the 1958 to 1962 period of training Tibetan freedom fighters at Camp Hale most everyone living in upper Eagle County where the camp was located as well as nearby Leadville, sitting fifteen miles south, were unaware these activities were going on. Numerous rumors spread about the camp but no one could guess its real function.

Leadville shrank from its silver boom days of yesteryear despite a brief growth spurt when soldiers of the 10th Mountain Division underwent nearby alpine training for the latter stages of WWII. After the 10th departed, a majority of the buildings were dismantled down to their foundation slabs. During the late 1940s and 1950s, the area was periodically used by the Army for winter warfare training including an instructor curriculum in 1953. During Exercise Ski Jump, from January to March 1954, Regimental Combat Team size training was conducted which involved both small and large unit maneuvers in a mountain environment. [75]

The Mountain & Cold Weather Training Command operated from 1952 to 1958, emphasizing downhill skiing, cross country trekking and back country survival skills. America had learned bitter lessons from Korea that not all conflicts took place in warm climates. Bill "Sarge" Brown was the tough first sergeant then for the Camp Hale segment rendering support in the back country to visiting Special Forces groups. Sarge Brown later went on to become Mountain Operations Manager for the nascent Vail Ski Area in 1962, located just twenty-two miles to the north. Mercy Trujillo and older brother David remember seeing the Green Beret soldiers many times at the Reno Restaurant in their nearby town of Red Cliff. Also, Charley Troxel and his siblings often hiked and collected moss rocks in the Camp Hale area, frequently finding spent ammunition shells and other remnants of alpine training. One time they came upon an old car pockmarked with bullet holes. [75, 82]

In 1957, co-author Deb Turnbull Devries was but five years old when she was taken with other kids on a school Christmas trip to Camp Hale. Initially excited to be going on an excursion, trepidation quickly set in when her school bus at Hale's main gate was boarded by armed soldiers. *What's happening? Are we in trouble?* were thoughts quickly racing her five-year-old mind. Camp Hale was still a well guarded facility during the 1950s. Her fears, however, dissipated in short order with the trip turning out to be quite enjoyable in what still remained of Camp Hale. It wouldn't be long after this event when the first group of Tibetans arrived at their newly constructed compound. So secret was the CIA training facility that no one the authors spoke to today knew what was going on or even knew someone who did. The cover was almost blown, however, when newly arrived Zeke Zilaitis, who had worked with Poe and Fosmire in Thailand, modified some five-inch rockets, with one veering off course and destroying a telegraph cable near the Climax Mine. Compensation was quickly and quietly paid to ensure that the secrecy lid stayed on. [41, 82]

Apparently at the time, signs were placed on Camp Hale's roads warning intruders to "Keep Out! Atomic Testing." Military police sent up from Fort Carson also extensively patrolled the perimeter with supposedly shoot-to kill orders. [50] In fact, the government even arranged for a brief article be posted in Colorado's Rocky Mountain News advising everyone of the atomic testing. It wasn't until many years later after the camp was fully deactivated that Trujillo, Troxel and the authors became aware this training had even been going on... nor did Robert Tresize, our high school teacher who fought in the Korea War know. In the early 1970s, many of us graduated from the same high school, located just 10 miles down the road, without ever having a clue. [82]

The training at Camp Hale was winding down. Tony Poe left near the end of 1960 but the biggest blow came when Tom Fosmire decided to join Roger McCarthy at the Tibet Task Force desk in Washington. Fosmire had bonded with the Tibetans more than any other CIA agent. He was with them from the early days of training and joined them at many an evening campfire, laughing and swapping stories. They regaled Fosmire with their annual trade caravans into India, surviving bandits and avalanches. Fosmire said, "They told me that when Tibet was free, they would take me on their biggest caravan ever." [44]

On the night before Fosmire was to leave, he assembled everyone to make the announcement of his departure.

> "Instantly, tears began to flow. Even when Mr. Tom assured us he would continue to be involved with the task force, we still cried like babies," said Mark the translator. Equally choked with emotion, Fosmire had to excuse himself, taking a twenty-minute walk to regain his composure. [44]

## Part Two (1954-1959)

Out of 259 Tibetans trained at Camp Hale and parachuted into Tibet, only 10% survived, either dying in combat or by taking their cyanide pills. Most all of them were enthusiastic, brave and funny.... they enjoyed telling and listening to tall tales around the evening campfire. [41]

The Tibetan resistance moved their camp to the Mustang area of Nepal after the U2 incident of 1960 barred airdrops over communist territory. It was led by Baba Yeshe, and suffering from political discord, embezzlement and a lack of weapons, ended up producing marginal results, with one notable exception. In October 1961, a group of Tibetan fighters from Mustang ambushed a Chinese jeep on the Xinjiang road. Ross, the group leader, took careful aim and fired into the first cab, killing the driver. Then, another Chinese male and female in a front seat were riddled with bullets, forcing the vehicles to a stop. As Ross approached to take photographs, gunfire suddenly erupted from the back of a truck but it was quickly silenced. [41, 44]

Checking the Jeep's contents, Ross removed a large leather document case which turned out to be a treasure trove detailing aspects of the Chinese-Soviet rift, problems the Chinese Army was having and full extent of suffering by the Chinese people from effects of the Great Leap Forward. Intelligence derived from the find put brief life into the Tibetan program but America soon became preoccupied with Vietnam and Laos. Tibet was summarily pushed down to the bottom of the government's priority list. The already reduced support was eventually cut off following Nixon's visit to China in early 1972. [42, 44]

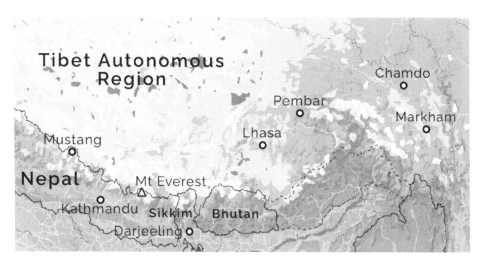

Southern Tibet (1950s & 1960s)

# The Butterfly Men

"Tending the stove fire, is like everything else associated with a harsh Peking winter, which was long, cold and dry. When the storms came from the Gobi Desert, the stove fires had to be carefully banked against the wind that blew so hard it leaped down the stove pipes and threatened to extinguish the flame. That was my only source of heat... for days I shivered." [6]

- John T. Downey (prison -year 6)

Tony Poe and Tom Fosmire had been working for Sea Supply in Bangkok for several years, being primarily involved with training aspects. The training program, which was originally started by Bill Lair, took place at several locations including Lopburi, Hua Hin and later Phitsanulak. With the coup in September 1957, the training program shut down with the PARU soldiers being restricted to base. The country's Army leader, Sarit Thanarat, didn't like highly trained paramilitary police outside army control so arrangements were made to absorb them into the military command. Nor did he like Thailand's involvement in the opium business which Phao, the exiled police chief controlled. During the coup hiatus, many CIA agents left Thailand while Poe and Fosmire would be urgently called to temporarily duty in Indonesia. Poe, receiving the notice, actually welcomed a break from police training. He also linked up with fellow agent, James Haase, who had previously worked for him in Korea. Haase recently was spending his time destroying incriminating agency documents in light of the

Thai coup... supposedly SEA Supply records involving matters other than simply training police recruits to parachute. [40]

Sumatra is mountainous and sitting right near the equator, it is also humid and fertile ground having an abundance of flora and fauna. In a unique attempt by the CIA to be creative, Poe and Haase's cover would be going in as professional entomologists. Essentially, butterfly collectors assigned to do research and catch some rare species in central Sumatra. They even had the requisite nets and documentation. [40]

On hand to meet them as their seaplane landed on Sumatra's Lake Singkarak was Pat Landry, who later became Bill Lair's assistant during the Laos secret war. A small group of PRRI rebels were also present as well. Poe and Haase promptly got to work that evening developing a detailed training syllabus which was completed by morning. As they were about to begin the initial instruction, not a single person showed up. Tony Poe, in characteristic manner, exclaimed, "Why the fuck did we even come here?" This beginning eventually became symbolic of how the Indonesian misadventure in general would later unfold. [40]

The PRRI was the rebel organization based in Padang, West Sumatra which in 1958 had declared its independence from the central Jakarta government. This included forming a cabinet with a prime minister and wrapping in fellow rebels, Permesta, on Sulawesi. The outlying islands felt the central government on Java was unresponsive and disconnected from the people. Organization, control and loyalties were problems that began manifesting from the start. Indonesia had a large and disparate population scattered across 17,000 islands encompassing Christians, Muslims, Hindus, Buddhists and even indigenous religions. Half of the country's population lived on Java and the Javanese had traditionally occupied most of the government posts. To make matters even more complex, were the slew of notable Indonesians vying for control and the many shipments of arms, ships and planes being sent in by the Philippines, CIA and even Chiang Kai-shek on Taiwan. [40, 81]

CIA air drops and strike missions were initially made from planes piloted by Poles, Czechs and even Romanians so as to maintain the CIA's cover of deniability. Indonesian airborne troops disrupted a major arms delivery to the PRRI leading the US to consider terminating use of eastern European flight crews. Tom Fosmire was with the Ostiary Group, as they were called, to assist in fusing and loading 500-lb bombs aboard the B-26s. On one particular mission, a bomber went down killing all onboard, including a Polish WWII ace. As Fosmire later commented, "It was okay to fight the Russians but the Poles did not want to fight little brown people." He further added, "Their heart simply was no longer in it." They went home and from then on, the CIA became directly involved with the flying of combat missions. [40]

Sukarno led the liberation of Indonesia from the Dutch in 1949 and was elected the nation's first president. After a tumultuous period with parliamentary democracy, he instituted the concept of "guided democracy": a more autocratic system which brought stability and included elements of the Communist Party of Indonesia. He also supported the Non-Aligned Movement, a 120-nation block neither aligned with the Communists nor the West. Because the Eisenhower administration, in particular the Dulles brothers, perceived the world in binary terms, non-alignment essentially implied pro-communist leanings and a proclivity to joining the communist camp. Meanwhile, near Ambon on the eastern region of the archipelago.... [40, 81]

> Allen Pope's B-26 bomber was closing in fast on the Naiko, a transport ship carrying a company of Ambonese troops headed home from Java. It had now slowed to pull into the dock. Pulling up sharply, Pope released his first bomb but it missed, dropping harmlessly into the bay.
>
> Captain Bouchati, skipper of the Naiko, screamed at his soldiers to fire back. The Bren machine gunners on deck also pointed skyward. This time, a relentless Pope was almost upon them for his second run. Now there would be no mistake.... BOOM! It was a bullseye hit right on the ship's engine room. Seventeen soldiers and crew were killed in the blast that day on the Naiko. [40]

Pope now looked towards the shore for other targets and almost hit a morning market but his last bomb found its mark on the ice factory. Satisfied overall, he headed back to base. The next day, he chased the transport Sawega which took evasive action upon seeing Pope's plane but as he swooped down, his rear gunner spotted a P-51 Mustang fighter on their tail. Pope's last bomb dropped into the sea, exploding forty meters behind the Sawega. The Mustang was being flown by Captain Ignatius Dewanto who desperately wanted to have the first air-to air combat kill in the Indonesian Air Force. Shadowing Pope's B-26 making its dive, Dewanto let loose his wing mounted 50 caliber Guns — Rat-A-Tat-Tat! - Rat-A-Tat-Tat!

At almost the same time, bullets coming up from the Sawega raked Pope's fuselage. The B-26 was hit multiple times until flames appeared in the cockpit. Pope rapidly climbed to get more altitude for a safer parachute jump. Leveling out at six thousand feet, the clam shell canopy was jettisoned and Pope jumped out. [40]

Captain Dewanto chased after the second B-26 flown by Pope's wingman, Connie Seigrist. Dewanto wanted a second round with these rebel bomber flyers but Siegrist broke off contact to fight another day. It wouldn't have been a match anyway in a dogfight with the highly maneuverable P-51. The Permesta rebels were down now to a single mid-range bomber which, unbeknownst to President Sukarno, was being flown and crewed by the CIA.

Handsome, daring and a somewhat arrogant young man of thirty years is the best way to describe Allen Pope. He took chances where most others would be curtailed by caution. He was also found tangled up with his parachute in a tree, having broken a leg, a result of hitting the tail section of his burning plane when bailing out. He was quickly apprehended and surprisingly had been carrying a full packet of incriminating information, including his Civil Air Transport (CAT) identity card, military separation file, and even the flight plans of his previous strikes. This was a flagrant violation of standard procedure for CAT and the CIA. But as Tom Fosmire later said, "Pope wasn't stupid." He believed that Pope knew about the capture of agents Downey and Fecteau back in 1952 and the ramifications of "going sterile." It allowed the CIA to disavow any connection or responsibility to them, resulting in their continued incarceration in China six years later. The agency felt protected but it was at the expense of the agents who had undertaken the risk. Pope reversed everything and while this angered his employer, he was cleverly able to leverage himself in later negotiations. [40, 81, 16]

However, that was easier said than done as he was held for several years under house arrest before being tried and given a death sentence. Around this time, the US had completely reversed its position opposing Sukarno and began courting him instead. Pope was a CAT pilot whose own flight records directly matched numerous bombings, including the Naiko transport ship where seventeen had died. He was ultimately given his freedom by Sukarno in return for ten Lockheed C-130 transport planes provided by the US. Allen Dulles, however, still did not acknowledge Downey and Fecteau whose only crime was they had been shot down on the wrong side of the Chinese border. [16]

The Eisenhower administration struggled with plotting a coherent course in it's dealing with Indonesia albeit some of the difficulty was of President Sukarno's doing. Because of Eisenhower's ardent anti-communism, he favored a divided country over a united one if united meant it being under communist rule. In August 1957, an interdepartmental committee on Indonesia was formed during a NSC meeting comprising the CIA, departments of State and Defense, and Joint Chiefs of Staff as members. They advocated that a dual approach be taken where covert means be used to strengthen anti-communist forces outside of Java, while also maintaining aid to the central government and non-communists within the military. By the time of Pope's capture, however, the presence of CIA advisors had already become an open secret and it became obvious that fighting communism was not a cause PRRI soldiers were willing to die for. A terse message was sent from Washington via Clark Air Base near Manila: "Cease all operations immediately and withdraw to the Philippines." [40, 16]

By 1959, the provision regarding intervention in outlying islands was removed from the committee's policy statement. The revised statement hinged on building better ties with the Indonesian armed forces. With 'egg now on his face', CIA Director Dulles would put his personal spin on how the CIA performed in Indonesia by awarding Pat Landry the Intelligence Star, the CIA's highest merit award. Tony Poe, Tom Fosmire and Roger McCarthy, during this timeframe, were called to work on the Tibetan Task Force, a seemingly more focused and inspiring endeavor. Pat Landry would make his presence known later in Laos, as the assistant to Bill Lair.

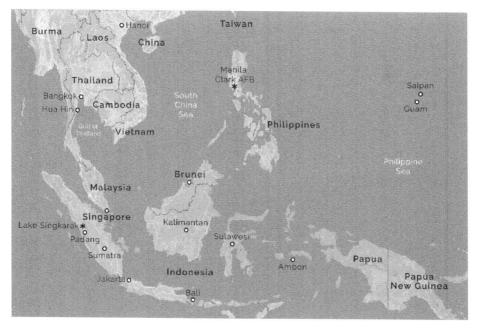

Indonesia (1950s)

# A Gathering of Storms

Following his capture by the Chinese and separation from Fecteau back in November 1952, Agent John Downey was transported to Shenyang, 400 miles away. He was shackled with leg irons, interrogated, and put in a solitary 5X8-foot prison cell. Downey was interrogated in four hour stretches up to 24 hours a day, sometimes going on for days at a time. Sleep deprivation was part of the psychological torture where he was only allowed to sleep for 30 minutes at a time. At times Downey was made to also stand endlessly for hours. After two years, he was reunited with Fecteau in 1954 for their show trial in Beijing. Fecteau was given a twenty-year sentence whereas Downey received life imprisonment. The Chinese figured that since Downey graduated from Yale, a more prestigious university, he must have been the group's leader. [6]

Zhou Enlai, after the trial, stated he would be willing to discuss release of the two agents and invited their families to visit. Secretary of State John Foster Dulles rejected the offer and forbade visits by the family. Yet again in 1957, Zhou Enlai offered to release Downey and Fecteau if the United States would allow American journalists to visit China. Once more, Dulles bluntly rejected the offer calling it an attempt at blackmail. It's believed by a number of authors and historians that Secretary Dulles' extreme animosity of Chinese Communists, coupled with his Calvinist faith, precluded the notion of cooperating with Zhou Enlai. Dulles passed away two years later, while Downey and Fecteau were essentially forgotten about... spending another fifteen years entrenched in the Chinese prison system. [6, 81]

As the late 1950s approached, the viability of the CIA sourcing heroin from LiMi's army of poppy growers had greatly diminished due to several factors. Futile attempts at invading Yunnan Province convinced President Truman to withdraw financial support. The Nationalist army's continued presence in Shan State had become a sore point with the Burmese government to the point of them taking up the matter with the United Nations. American denials reached a limit and so began the effort to repatriate Nationalist soldiers and their families back to Taiwan. When Operation REPAT was finally completed in March 1953, Civil Air Transport transported 5,583 soldiers, 1,040 dependents and an assortment of machine guns and mortars back to Taiwan. Some Nationalist soldiers still remained but opium cultivation had been greatly diminished.

The CIA kept an eye out for another potential opium source; more importantly, someone who could solve other pressing agency issues at the time. Issues such as the agency's concern that communists would take over Laos. Vang Pao, a Meo tribesman and military leader, came to their attention. The Meo, or Hmong as they preferred to be called, were a sizable indigenous tribe living in the highland areas of Laos. Typically, the Hmong don't recognize national borders by having a presence also in Vietnam, Thailand and China, the land of their ancestors. Their relationship with Ming, Mongol and Han rulers in China over the centuries alternated between peace and warfare, leading many Hmong to escape southward into the Indochina region. They had no great love for the Han Chinese, remembering the latter destroying everything in their path, including homes, their agricultural land and even desecrating the graves of their Hmong deceased. [36, 43, 81]

The Hmong did survive, raising cattle, goats and pigs to supplement their diet of rice and corn. The drier, somewhat cooler highlands climate was also conducive, of course, to growing the opium poppy as their main cash crop. The Hmong would often grow the plants between their stalks of corn which would be harvested first. Processing the poppy plant is a multistage project which can be easily converted onsite to become morphine, a powerful pain medication. It was normally used by the Hmong for stomach ailments and was also applied in putty form to soldiers' wounds. From the morphine comes heroin base, usually requiring a lot of water, certain industrial chemicals and some lab equipment. Hydrochloride acid is then required to convert the heroin's crude base into refined heroin. Not that many Hmong smoked opium and even less became addicted to it, so it never became a societal problem for them. [36, 43, 46, 70]

The CIA needed a sizable army of anti-communists and found it with the Hmong under the leadership of General Vang Pao. Pao's opium supply chain was long in both time and distance. The CIA's Technical Services Division got to work mechanizing and streamlining the process by using portable heroin processing facilities and even trained some Hmong how to operate them. Costs were cut immensely, favorably impacting profits. Shipment of opium product was simply listed on the manifests as "diverse." The CIA later provided Pao with two C-47s to form his own airline which was nicknamed "Air Opium." Some actually considered Vang Pao a lessor player in the opium business, the bigger one being General Ouane Rattikone, who as the Royalist Commander in Chief, was Vang Pao's boss. [36, 43]

Aside from distribution to international markets, a burgeoning regional market was ready made given the influx of American soldiers ramping up in mid 1960s. Downtrodden areas near military posts in Vietnam became easy outlets for different grades of heroin that transited through Laos next door. [36]

Vietnam in the meantime, was undergoing growing pains of its own as the Geneva Conference in 1954 left matters unresolved. The plan was for partitioned North and South Vietnam to hold elections within two years, the ultimate goal being unification of the country. In the meantime, the Viet Minh were to vacate the South just as the French had agreed to leave North Vietnam. When Ngo Dinh Diem who took over as Premier in 1954, he reneged. He is noted, however, for certain early accomplishments such as putting down the Binh Xuyen gangster organization in Saigon, the Cao Dai armed sect and gaining limited international recognition for South Vietnam. Early successes would prove to fleeting and as time went on, Diem a zealous Catholic, would become more oppressive, dictatorial and lacking in popular support.

In 1954, Colonel Edward Lansdale, acting largely on behalf of the Dulles brothers, was brought in following success against the communist insurgents in the Philippines. He would also become one of the few CIA people whom Diem actually trusted. By January 1955, Lansdale began the centerpiece of Diem's national security initiative called the Civil Action Program. While organized and funded by the CIA, it ultimately failed in its objectives to win the hearts and minds of the rural population. Diem soon also alienated large segments of the armed forces, the rural population and even the Buddhists. Suspecting that many Buddhists would vote for Viet Minh, which continued remaining in the South, Diem had the upcoming 1956 election rigged, supposedly winning by a landslide. Viet Minh ranks swelled by 1957, with typically non-communist sympathizers, as a result of Diem's repressive policies and pervasive corruption. By 1957, Lansdale's tenure and waning influence on Diem had run its course and he left Saigon for Washington. The facade of democracy was masking a reality preoccupied by the pressing needs for internal security. Needs made progressively worse by the leader in charge. [34, 81]

While the political skies were darkening over Vietnam, Laos was dealing with its own set of problems. Since the gaining their independence from France in December 1954, things were relatively fine with Souvanna Phouma in 1956 beginning his second term as Prime Minister. The communist Pathet Lao were led by Souvanna's half-brother, Souphanouvang and by 1958, neutralist Souvanna was forced to resign by the Royalists.

Back in 1954, the Vietnamese had formed a special Military Adviser Group to aid the Pathet Lao. Known as Group 100, its objective was to establish a military and political force that could stand on its own. In return, the Pathet Lao allowed North Vietnam in 1959 to construct the Truong Son Strategic Supply Route through Laos which would be continually improved and better known as the Ho Chi Minh Trail. That same year, one of several tri-coalition governments were attempted to be formed but efforts proved to be problematic. In the summer, Green Berets soldiers began training the Royal Laotian Army under Operation Hotfoot due to the perceived Pathet Lao/North Vietnamese threat. In 1960, a Captain Kong Le, professed Lao neutralist, staged a coup in Vientiane using his parachute battalion. By December that year, the CIA working with Thailand Prime Minister Sarit, launched a counter-coup committing the Thai Police Aerial Reinforcement Unit (PARU) to be used in Laos. The North Vietnamese Army, greatly escalating tensions, moved its own troops into northern Laos the following year. [23, 24, 61]

The turmoil in Laos quickly came to the forefront of Kennedy's new administration. Actually, it was Kennedy's first foreign policy crisis with him needing to decide between taking unilateral military intervention or seeking a cease-fire and neutralization. In July 1962, another conference in Geneva reached a Declaration of Neutrality for Laos. That declaration stipulated a coalition government headed again by Souvanna be set up, prohibited military bases, and called for a withdrawal of all regular and irregular military troops. It was all for naught as most every side violated the agreement from the very start... the North Vietnamese left 7,000 troops in Laos, China and the Soviet Union continued supplying the Pathet Lao with military support, the US began a bombing campaign and the Pathet Lao renewed their attacks. [23, 24]

Just when things appeared to have quieted down in the Taiwan Straits, another crisis develops. In August 1958, the Chinese Army (PLA) began shelling Quemoy and other islands occupied by Nationalist forces. This was quickly followed by a brief naval battle and attempted amphibious landing by the PLA around Dongding Island. The US sent the larger 155mm howitzers to Quemoy, resulting in even more artillery duels with the PRC. A month or so later under the secret, Operation Black Magic, the US retrofitted Nationalist F-86 fighter jets with the newly developed Sidewinder air-to-air missiles. That provided the Nationalists a distinct edge over MIG-15 and MiG-17s, until the advantage was lost when an unexploded missile lodged into a Mig-17. The Soviets could now reverse engineer the Sidewinder and make one on their own. At a later point during the three-month long conflict, the Joint Chiefs of Staff would recommend the use of nuclear weapons... as a last resort. [70]

# PART THREE (1960-1966)

# Building Up Momentum

Tony Poe and Pat Landry were among the first agents to arrive in Laos as was Jack Shirley in 1961 and 1962. Poe took over site location and building of airstrips, known as Lima Sites, in the Plain of Jars area of northeast Laos. In hilly and thickly tropical Laos, multiple short landing strips became the preferred means of transport and delivery, aside from airdrops. The Helio Courier and Pilatus Porter's short take off and landing (STOL) aircrafts were considered ideal for the high altitude, short mountain airstrips of the region. The airstrips were built in varying lengths and were seldom flat or straight. One source was known to comment, "Some strips defied all the safety rules of even military aviation." [58]

Landry became an assistant to Bill Lair and they'd both move into a small, nondescript building called AB-1 at Udorn Royal Thai Air Base, fifty miles south of Vientiane. Udorn also housed the headquarters of Air America, the airline covertly owned and working for the CIA. Before the change to their present name they had been operating there since 1955 as Civil Air Transport. In 1961, President Kennedy believed Thailand would be overrun by the North Vietnamese after victory in the Battle of Luang Namtha in Laos so US Marine forces were sent in. They were withdrawn from Udorn in mid-1962 when things calmed down a bit.

The 432nd Tactical Reconnaissance Wing came aboard the base to provide needed intelligence gathering for both military and agency purposes. Unarmed RF-4 Phantom IIs would have three rotating cameras in the nose cone and be escorted on sorties by other armed Phantoms. Udorn would become the nerve center for Operation Momentum where Lair's trained Thai PARU would teach Hmong hill tribesmen in the ways of guerrilla warfare. This began January 1961 and just four days afterwards, they scored their first combat victory by destroying a unit of fifteen Pathet Lao during a prepared ambush. The training was solid and PARU turned out to be perfect trainers, having pervious experience of working with indigenous people and speaking a very similar language. Later, the Thai organization, Headquarters 333, would also set up their offices at Udorn to coordinate Thai soldiers committed to operations in Laos. [51, 81]

The early success of Momentum led to its expansion countrywide and emulation by the Green Berets in Operation Pincushion, which was centered on the Ho Chi Minh Trail in southern Laos. Pincushion was an outgrowth of Operation White Star where the Green Berets had earlier been training both regular and irregular Laotian forces, often with French assistance. Operation Pincushion, however, largely failed when the Geneva Conference of 1962 required withdrawal of US military forces from Laos. Another lesson taken away from Pincushion is caution about mixing fighters from different ethnic tribes who might not get along. Tony Poe would have this very same problem of ethnic infighting later in northwest Laos. [23, 24]

For a small country, Laos is a veritable melting pot. There are almost fifty different ethnicities forming 160 groups speaking 82 dissimilar languages. Add to this mix of languages, Chinese and certain unclassified dialects. The three million Lao living in the lowlands, where rice is mostly cultivated, make up slightly over half the population. The Hmong make up almost ten percent of the population, largely keeping to themselves in the highlands. Originally from China, they can trace their history back almost five thousand years but were relative newcomers to Laos, escaping Chinese persecution and ongoing conflict. Making up half that number are also the Sino-Tibetans who, over time, would venture south into the region. [81]

The Hmong in Laos have divergent loyalties from their Hmong counterparts in Vietnam as they are strongly anti-Vietnamese and opposed to communism. Factors considered crucial for lending their support to active resistance. The

## Part Three (1960-1966)

Hmong are Animists, believing that natural objects and phenomena have souls that exist outside their physical bodies. Animism, incidentally, believe all righteous deities are saviors and for that reason, they are easily convertible to Christianity. When it comes to their character, one author noted:

> "The Hmong are known for their exceptional honesty. If a promise is given, it will always be fulfilled... even if years later." [57]

> Agent Vint Lawrence, who was initially assigned to Laos in 1962, describes them best: [46, 78]

> "The Hmong strike me as a truly esoteric, wild, marvelous group of people. I mean, the men are extraordinarily handsome, but in a very carved, Oriental manner. They're incredibly strong and while not being big people you would occasionally see a six-foot man" [58]

> Lawrence would go on further to say...

> "They had incredible endurance and could walk through the jungle faster than anybody I knew. The real local people who never wore shoes, their little toes, genetically, had moved from a point of being parallel to the other toes to being almost at a right angle. So when they went up a trail, their toes were virtually prehensile, and they would actually grab... they could move up a trail with a speed that was truly frightening, and they could walk for days." [58]

Back when the calendar flipped to 1961, Bill Lair met Vang Pao for the first time. He remembers a man about five foot five with a rounded face and ready smile. The appearance, while pleasant, belied the character of the man. Out of a class of eighty at the police academy, Vang ranked number one, the only ethnic person in a class of Lao lowlanders who believed minorities were inferior. Vang later showed a determination and ruthlessness under the French when he hunted down and killed a communist captain, while drawing no quarter. Joining the Royal Laos Army, he rose to the rank of Major by 1959. Just two years later, Lair could see the way Vang ran his camp and the discipline of his men who followed his every dictate. Simply put, he ran a tight ship. The Hmong fighters would need a leader of their own cloth, but also one who garnered the respect of the Laos monarchy. Someone who could unite all the clans and energize recruitment to bolster the ranks. The right man for that job seemed to be Vang Pao. However, first... [51]

Bill Lair, perhaps knowing the situation involving the CIA and the Tibetans, bluntly asked Vang Pao:

> "Neither the Laotian government nor the US government could support a Hmong independence movement. What do your people want to do?"

> Vang thought for a brief moment and then he answered:

> "The Hmong want to keep their way of life and follow their own leaders. They want to fight the communists. They will follow me and I am loyal to the king".

> That was good enough for Bill Lair. [51]

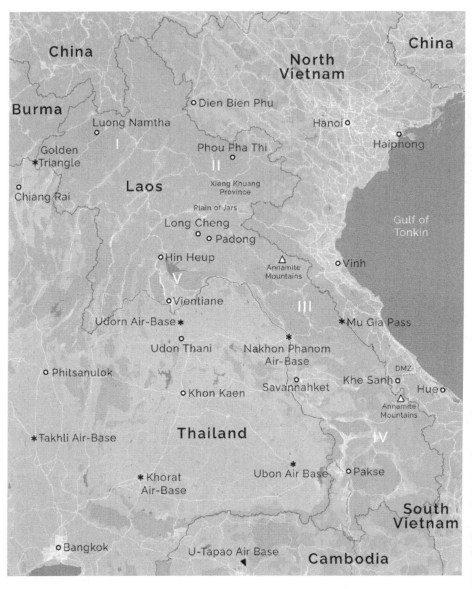

Southeast Asia (1960s & 1970s)

# Frog on the Moon

"Even in my own corridor, I never saw my neighbor inmates. Each one of us was fed, exercised, and taken to the toilet in his turn. I kept track of the others' comings and goings by the sliding of bolts and the snapping of padlocks. I knew Fecteau was nearby because I heard his cough occasionally and had come to recognize the sound of his shuffle when he was taken from his cell to the toilet." [6]

- John T. Downey (prison -year 7)

Bill Lair was working late in his Vientiane office one night in early March 1961.

About to wrap up for the night, he began to hear gunfire: POW, POW followed by RAT-TAT-TAT machine gun bursts, with an occasional BOOM from a mortar round that decided to chime in. [51]

*What the Hell!?*, he thought. Then the electricity went off. *Is this another coup?* now concerned, he ran outside to take a look. The police, soldiers and civilians all seemed to be involved in the chaotic shooting.

"What is going on?" Lair loudly asked a well-dressed Lao woman running by, shooting her pistol towards the sky.

## Part Three (1960-1966)

> "The Frog is eating the Moon! The Frog is eating the Moon!" she Screamed, while firing off another round. [51]

A partial lunar eclipse was taking place and the shadowy disc covering the moon was passing across to slowly reveal the lunar surface again. The people thought the Cosmic Frog was eating the moon and then began disgorging it after being shot at. The Laotians were greatly relieved that the moon appeared again in the night sky. Heading home and passing stretchers bearing people hit by errant bullets, Bill Lair felt relieved it wasn't another coup. [51]

The Lao can be quite superstitious, particularly the indigenous people. The Thai and Vietnamese can be as well. Sometimes Buddhism takes on a more dominant role and other times it is Animism, a belief that spirits underlie all living things. The communists downplay the role of religion in people's lives but old beliefs can still run deep. Sometimes propaganda and psychological warfare can effectively play on those beliefs.

The psychological war in Laos consisted of a multitude of organizations working together to prevent the overthrow of the Royal Laos Government by communist forces. When it came to PSYOPS in Laos, the primary agencies involved were the US Information Agency, US Agency for International Development, Military Assistance Command - Vietnam and, of course, the CIA. The Air Force, specifically the 7th PSYOP Group based in Okinawa, produced the content and provided the means of delivery as did later Air America. One of the central problems in Laos was that illiteracy was quite widespread so messages had to be portrayed in picture form, often using cartoons. Use of radio broadcasting, and loudspeaker announcements under the Loudmouth Program was often accompanied by playing Wagner's "Ride of the Valkyries." The dropping of leaflets from planes under Operation Litterbug was yet another delivery mechanism that was frequently utilized. [66]

> "Come on Down. Surrender and meet Bubble Gum!"

This was one of the more creative messaging done by the CIA. The leaflet featured a naked lady in high heels in one of Vientiane's notorious taverns. It seems Bubble Gum was actually one of the better known "ladies of the night" offering her image for a good cause. Not sure how effective the message was in inducing surrenders (or in bringing Bubble Gum any more business) but not everyone was taken in. Pilots, in slow flying planes, would routinely be shot at while making leaflet airdrops. One waving a few Bubble Gum leaflets complained, "I'm risking my life out here in enemy country to drop this !?" Guess he never met Bubble Gum. [66]

Many PSYOPS flights focused exclusively on the Ho Chi Minh Trail. One example of leaflets dropped in the vicinity of the trail, in Vietnamese, said:,

> "Go back to Hanoi. Go back to your wife or girlfriend
> Have a good life." [66]

After a particular B-52 bombing run, they'd fly back over the same area to assess bomb damage, now dropping leaflets which said:

> "Hey, I told you so!"

Most propaganda information was more serious and direct. Some played upon superstitions and local folklore. For instance, in Central Vietnam, a particularly sad yet chilling PSYOPS broadcasted voices as if pleading with enemy soldiers to give up fighting. Many Vietnamese believe that if one dies and is buried far from home, the soul would wander aimlessly in the afterworld.

> "My friends, I have come back to let you know that I am dead!" a disembodied voice exclaimed in Vietnamese.

> "It's hell... I am in hell! Please don't end up like me. Go home, friends, before it's too late!" [66]

The recording was accompanied by sobbing, wailing and occasional shrieks from various voices, including those of children.

## Part Three (1960-1966)

Many PSYOPS themes appeared to have limited impact on achieving the results being sought. The Pathet Lao and North Vietnamese were generally a resilient people who were used to making sacrifices. While attempts to undermine Pathet Lao political initiatives were successful during the early years, communists' intensified indoctrination would later negate the effect of many PSYOP themes. Captured enemy soldiers often remarked that they simply used the PSYOP printed material to roll their cigarettes or for toilet paper. [66]

In addition to superstitions attempting to influence lunar eclipses, more scientifically based endeavors were made to affect the weather. For instance, rainmaking in Vietnam and Laos, which in the latter was formally called Operation Pop-Eye. The stated program objective was "intended to reduce traffic ability along infiltration routes." It was also considered experimental and was run by the CIA later using Air Force planes. Before the focus shifted to the Ho Chi Minh trail in the mid-1960s, Air America provided their small Beechcraft planes rigged up to spray silver iodide. The cloud seeding along the Ho Chi Minh Trail was intended to make it muddy enough to impair movement of North Vietnamese troops and supplies, particularly during monsoon season. No telling how successful it really was against the resilient North Vietnamese, however. Pop-Eye did have some ability to disrupt enemy radars which guided their surface to air missiles, a continuing problem for US pilots. However, Operation Pop-Eye was not able to create any heavy flooding and program administrators admitted that mistakes were often made along the way.

> "Once we mistakenly dumped up to seven inches of rain on one of our own Special Forces camps," an official admitted. [81]

# Sigma and Sierra

"On May 1, 1961, their ground forces crossed the border, heading towards the capital, just thirty miles away. Jets and bombers were pounding the airfields but with marginal effect. To protect the city, help from the United States was urgently needed which America provided pursuant to its treaty obligations. The US responded with its tactical air and naval force on the second day. Still, the enemy drove unabated towards the capital with its reinforced armored division and tactical air support.

"The ground forces continued their relentless drive despite sustaining heavy losses to its air forces. To prevent capitulation of the capital, the United States now decided to use nuclear weapons on the enemy troops and their airfields.

"On the third day, the nuclear bombs were actually dropped destroying the bases but were unable to stop the vanguard of the ground forces which had gotten too close to the city. A second nuclear strike was made that afternoon against the rear echelon units but by then it was simply too late, the bulk of the enemy forces had now entered the capital!" [69]

Fortunately, this war did not actually happen and nuclear weapons weren't used. This was a wargame scenario developed by M. G. Weiner for the Rand

## Part Three (1960-1966)

Corporation in 1959. The concept of wargaming have been around a long time with modern gaming starting with Prussia. After they defeated France in the Franco-Prussian War in 1871, many other countries soon adopted the concept of strategizing the moves of warfare. The Rand Corporation began in 1955 with the Sierra Project simulating conflicts in South East, the Far East and the Middle East with limited war. Limited war means air, sea, ground and logistics actions also involving political and economic aspects. As Weiner envisaged, the Red Team were the Communists, the Blue was the US and its allies, whereas the neutral Control Team managed the gameplay to ensure relevance and adherence to scenario objectives. Each team's move, which might take up to a day to decide, was passed through the Control Team. As Weiner said of the gaming exercise,

> "It possess no prophetic qualities. It's representation of the future is as much open to challenge as that of any other analytic technique. It consists basically of description or observation that is projected into the future." [69]

The Sierra games are considered "true" war games since they include a large number of variables than simply military strategy and tactical inputs. They start with the events preceding the outbreak of war and continue through the war, only stopping at a predetermined point.

The Sigma war games began in 1962, focusing on the Vietnam War, and continued with one or two game periods every year until 1967. These classified games were staged by the Joint War Games Agency within the Pentagon, having high ranking officials and simulations solicited from the State Department, CIA and various military agencies. The major conclusion drawn from the first game, called Sigma-62, was that American intervention would not be successful. [69, 80]

Sigma-63, in the following year, considered the prospect of a massive Chinese intervention as had happened during the Korean War. It also weighed the influence of adverse domestic and international public opinion on the war.

William Sullivan, the US ambassador to Laos, was an active participant of Sigma-63 gameplay.

Probably the most significant simulation was the second one of two held during 1964. That session occurred just a month following the Gulf of Tonkin Resolution in early August when America scaled up its involvement in the war. Of the many variables, it now additionally dealt with the use of nuclear weapons, presumably the tactical version, similar to Weiner's scenario in 1959. The Blue Team would end up having disagreements over the use of nuclear bombs. Apparently, the Commander of Pacific Forces, during the simulation, had requested use of tactical nuclear weapons but was denied. The simulation had the US face off against a Chinese division in northern Laos, after first conducting conventional air strikes against them. One of the major take-aways from Sigma-II 64 was the mistaken belief in the beneficial value of a robust air campaign,

> "Going into the games, there was a basic assumption that a gradually escalating aerial campaign could lead to a U.S. victory. The actual conclusion instead was that bombing would stiffen the North Vietnamese resolve and will to resist." [80]

Khe Sanh, a US Marine combat post twelve miles from the Laos border and fourteen miles south of the demilitarized zone found itself under relentless siege for five months, beginning late January 1968. The two regiments faced continual artillery bombardments and infantry assaults by up to three North Vietnamese divisions. In many respects, it was reminiscent of the French defense of Dien Bien Phu, fourteen years previously, and attracted worldwide attention. After ordering a massive bombing campaign to defend the base at all costs, General Westmoreland began considering his other options. [81]

It's noteworthy that Sigma II-64 dealt with the issue of tactical nuclear weapons despite not being favorably considered. However, just three years later, during the Battle of Khe Sanh, their use was not only contemplated but actually being planned for. With the approval of the Commander of Pacific Forces, General Westmoreland put together a top-secret program called Fracture Jaw. It included propositioning nuclear weapons in South Vietnam in case their use might be needed as a last resort, a situation now being faced in Khe Sanh.

Presumably these would be tactical nuclear weapons for use on the battlefield. The B61 nuclear bomb approached peak production by 1968 with 3,155 being made. It was "variable yield", meaning an operator could select the size of blast he wanted, depending on the situation, from a low of 300 tons to a high of 50 kilotons, which is over three times as powerful as the bomb dropped on Hiroshima. Importantly, being almost 12-feet long and looking like a streamlined missile, the B61 could be deployed on a number of combat aircraft from bombers to attachment on the bomb-rack under certain fighter planes. [80, 81]

When President Johnson found out about Fracture Jaw, he became extremely upset, ordering that it to be shut down immediately. Johnson feared an escalation into a much wider war with the Chinese entering as they had done in Korea back in 1950. During the early 1950s, the Joint Chiefs of Staff were also quick to recommend use of the nuclear option to the National Security Council. Defense officials often talk about an "escalation ladder" where one country's action forces another to escalate the situation. Tactical nuclear weapons, therefore, are simply the rung separating a conventional conflict from a strategic nuclear war and the US is not the only country having them. To this day, no tactical nuclear weapon has ever been used in combat and there is good reason why a civilian is Commander in Chief of the US military. They have a vantage point more expansive than the immediate field of conflict, a perspective including the likelihood of unwanted escalation. [80, 81]

The years of Sigma games after 1964, dealt with de-escalation and ending of the Vietnam War. The Sigma II-64 gameplay is said to have paralleled actual events in many regards, such as North Vietnam shelling Da Nang and Bien Hoa airfields to counter American increased bombing, that General Nguyen Khanh would be pressured out of office in early 1965 and the mining of Haiphong harbor in 1972. [81]

Historian H. R. McMaster, differed from the opinions of Weiner, calling the Sigma war game results "eerily prophetic". In almost all Sigma simulations, the final outcome was either a communist win, or a stalemate which led to protests in the US. The issue comes down to the value derived from the gaming process itself since it appears minimal credence was placed on final results to influence US war policy. [81]

# Big Brother Watching

The Berlin Airlift had been completed a year previously when East German government took advantage of those low flying American aircraft passing over their sector. Max Troeger, living near Leipzig, saw two overflying his farm one afternoon and the next day read an article published by the East German press about potato beetles devastating crops. Naturally, it made for great disinformation that the Americans were trying to stall the economic recovery of East Germany by ruining their food supply. The propaganda machine revved up in full swing producing posters, even ones showing little beetles wearing US helmets and boots dropping out of the sky. School children throughout East Germany were tasked to hit the fields after class to collect the squishy insects and their larvae for later disposal. Of course, the only problem with propaganda is the truth and rational people willing to accept the truth. The Ministry of Agriculture, packed with politicians rather than scientists, saw a way to protect their own failings. Failings that included lacking sufficient pesticide supplies to control the pests which were a known scourge to European farmers going back to the late 19th century. [81]

In early 1950, when the beetle scare was taking place, the Ministry for State Security was also formed in East Germany. More commonly known as the Stasi, it would become one of the world's most oppressive security agencies, permeating all aspects of German Democratic Republic (GDR) life. The organization was vast, when including also their extensive network of informers, it's estimated they had a Stasi agent for every 6.5 East German residents. By comparison, the Nazis during the war had a Gestapo for every 2,000 people. Schools, universities and hospitals were highly infiltrated as was industrial factories depending on their size and products made. Every apartment building required at least one informant living on the premises. Tiny holes were drilled into hotel and apartment walls, sometimes even bathrooms, where camera surveillance could take place. [94]

The Main Reconnaissance Administration, (HVA), in 1957 was set up as the foreign intelligence arm of the Stasi, around the same time that Stasi became independent from the KGB. It was independence in name only as the latter remained deeply involved, often using Stasi as a proxy for their own worldwide activities. Stasi methods and organizational structure was originally patterned after the Soviet KGB and in turn was exported to other countries such as Ethiopia, Angola, Yemen, Mozambique, Ghana and, of course, Cuba. Those countries often sent their security agents to the GDR for specialized training. The HVA section, under Markus Wolf, fully penetrated the West German government and was known to be a financial supporter of the Red Army Faction terrorist group, known for killing dozens of West Germans.

In January 1961, Sigrid Ruhrdanz gave birth to their only child, a baby boy. It was a difficult delivery, requiring an emergency caesarean. Young Torsten was lucky to be alive as he suffered a ruptured diaphragm during delivery. His stomach and oesophagus were damaged; there was inflammation and internal bleeding, so the doctors operated immediately. While Torsten remained in Westend Hospital, Sigrid and husband Harmut had to get permission each time from the Ministry of Health to bring in medicines and special formula. The Ruhrdanz's lived in East Berlin whereas the hospital was located on the west side of the city. In late July 1961, there was no wall up but cross-border flow was still controlled and at midnight August 12th, the wall went up, albeit initially only barb wire. Sigrid returned to the Ministry but was refused the medicine and formula; permission to cross over was also refused.

> "Please, my son needs this. Without it, he may die" Sigrid pleaded "If your son is as sick as all that," the callous Ministry official told her. 'it would be better if he did.'"

## Part Three (1960-1966)

So began Sigrid's multi-year ordeal of trying to be with her son. She was able to visit Torsten a couple times at Westend but now has had enough and tries to escape from East Berlin using an ill-fated passport scheme. People were arrested. In 1963, the idea of tunneling out was suggested but the tunnel soon became flooded. The Stasi are now onto Sigrid and her husband and they begin following them.

> "In the morning when I went to work, there'd be someone close behind me," she says. "If I go in to Alexanderplatz to do some shopping, a man would come with me from my door, onto the bus and train and then home again. They changed personnel, but there was always someone there: they wanted us to feel it.'"

Things were about to get worse....

***

Totalitarian regimes and organizations typically have a leader who shapes the organization with his own beliefs and often in his own likeness. Those loyal quickly kowtow to the person while dissenters, be they real or imagined, are eliminated. Before long, a pervasive climate of fear and impunity contaminates the air. Such was the case with Stalin and Mao, including their subordinate security agencies. With the Stasi, it was Erich Mielke. He was self-centered, unprincipled and humorless but nevertheless very intelligent. His actions were driven by doing whatever was necessary for him to build and remain in power. With Mielke, the typical authoritarian process is no different.

Following the end of World War II in 1945, Erich Mielke returned to the Soviet Zone of occupied Germany, helping to organize a Marxist-Leninist satellite state under the Socialist Unity Party (SED). The Stasi was founded in February 1950, with Wilhelm Zaisser as its first Minister of State Security and Mielke as deputy. During the 1950s and 1960s, Mielke led the program of forcibly creating collectivized farms from East Germany's family-owned farms, sending a flood of refugees to West Germany. [94]

Until about 1955, many of the people arrested as enemies of the state were turned over to the Soviets, who then shipped them off to the Gulag. This was particularly true of fellow communists who disagreed with the SED leadership. There was no room for dissension to SED's creation or to its policies. The Stasi and the Soviet secret police employed every method of mental and physical brutality to cleanse the state of its enemies. Kidnapping of anticommunists from West Berlin took place almost on a weekly basis between 1945 and early 1960s with many simply disappearing without a trace. [94]

The year 1957 rolls around and Erich Mielke takes over as head of the Ministry of State Security. The Stasi's recruitment and deployment of secret informants became a science under Mielke after dissemination of his Richtlinie Manual. The top-secret document outlined mechanisms to surveil the population, down to every minute detail. Stasi officers were assigned quotas for recruiting informers and each officer supervised at least 30 regular informers. Some informers were as young as twelve years old with the oldest being eighty-nine. [94]

Mielke also oversaw the construction of the Berlin Wall in 1961 and was known to co-sign the orders for guards to fatally shoot East Germans who attempted to escape. He remained as the head of the feared Stasi until the reunification of Germany decades later. To him, every foreigner was a potential enemy who harbored evil intent. The Stasi's paranoia was pronounced and pervasive... and behind it all was the face of Erich Mielke. [94]

\*\*\*

One day, two men who had been trailing Sigrid Ruhrdanz finally stopped her and asked to see her ID. As she was about to retrieve it from her purse, they hustled her into a nearby black limousine. She knew right then they were Stasi. Her interrogation at Stasi headquarters lasted an astonishing twenty-two hours.

> "I understand your son finds himself in enemy territory. From our information, it appears that he is very ill," the snide, portly interrogator said.
>
> "Would you like to see your son?'

## Part Three (1960-1966)

She thought, *what sort of a question was that?* 'Yes, sir," she replied"

> "That can be arranged. We would only ask that, while
> you are in West Berlin, you arrange to meet up with your
> young friend, Michael Hinze. The two of you could go
> for a stroll in the park ... you can leave the rest to us."
> [95]

They were going to use her as a lure to kidnap Michael Hinze. Sigrid knew Hinze would trust her implicitly and come to a meeting in the park, and when they arrived to shove him into a vehicle, she would have to turn her back, walking away as if nothing happened. Hinze was the brave young student who had put together the passport scheme, helping many to freedom before the Stasi took steps requiring a certain stamp on the passport. [95]

Sigrid knew that if she accepted, they would have her soul, the cost to be paid for a visit to her critically ill son. She would be in their clutches, psychologically, forever. So she refused. At that time, she felt that it was the right decision... and even later as well. "I could always say to myself that I did not make myself guilty. I can sleep at night with what I have done," she said. [95]

There were, of course, ramifications. Sigrid and her husband never saw the charges placed against them, let alone the trial judgement. Yet they were sentenced to four years hard labor and taken to the notorious Hohenschönhausen prison to serve out their time. In August 1964, the couple were bought free for 40,000 Deutschmarks from the West German government. However, instead of being released into West Berlin to be with their baby, they were simply discarded on the street in the East without any papers. Of the thousands of people released for money over the years to the West, they were among the few cases to be shown such inhumanity. [95]

When he was five years old, Torsten was finally released from Westend Hospital and allowed to return to his family in East Germany. He was small, hunched over and his limbs crooked and yet he was also smart and polite. He did not recognized Sigrid as his mother. Torsten didn't even know what a mother was nor had he ever experienced the warmth of a loving family. He only knew of doctors and nurses in white clothing, living his first five years of life in a sterile institution. [95]

# The Tunnel Rats

They told her to meet at the pub at 7:30pm on Schonholzer Strasse. Her contact would be a well-dressed young woman who would sit down ordering coffee precisely at that time. Other patrons were ordering drinks and coffees but she spotted the woman who briefly shot her a glance, then got up grabbing her pack of cigarettes as if to step outside for a smoke. They followed, but not too closely. Once outside, the young woman looked toward the West Berlin side of the border and spotted a small white sheet hanging from a fourth floor apartment window. It's the all-clear signal that no "Vopos" or East German VolksPolizei, were near them on the East side of the border. [93]

She quickly mentioned the secret password, then followed the young woman a couple blocks down the poorly lit street to a shabby tenement at No. 7 Schonholzer. By order of the East German police, all tenements near the border were to have their front doors locked at 8pm. It would stay locked but if a refugee arrived, they could rely on someone on the inside to unlock and then relock the door. A few light taps on the door let's them in as they proceeded across the vacant lobby to a door leading down to the basement. In the far corner of the basement was a small hole in the floor, rigged up with a lamp just inside to provide necessary lighting. They were promptly directed over to the corner....[93]

> "Almost as if in a trance, and with no alternative but to trust the stranger, she passed her child to a pair of hands in the tunnel and then, in her new dress and nylons, climbed in herself. After crawling for a spell, she

lost her shoes, the dim yet adequate lamps illuminating the dark chamber." [93]

The tunnel was dank and tight, less than 3 by 3 feet and shaped like a triangle — very easy for anyone to get claustrophobic and due to Berlin's sandy soil, the constant fear of an entombing cave-in never escaped her mind. She and others had to be absolutely quiet as the East German police had embedded listening devices on the ground above. Were it not for the illumination and her faith at the end that there'd actually be an exit, she would be hesitant to proceed. She soon wondered what was above her: was she now underneath the Berlin Wall? Under the Death Strip? At long last, after crawling through puddles and dirt, she could hear voices from the other end with the light becoming noticeably brighter. [93]

Finally, a ladder came into view. It was slanted at an angle upwards towards the exit... just another fifteen steps up that ladder. Her thoughts turned to her baby daughter who was near the outlet, remarkably composed and quiet, being held by one of the helpers. Eveline had scrapes on her knees and hands, her dress was wet and torn but she and little Annett had finally made their way to freedom. Sweet freedom. [93]

The year of Eveline Schmidt's escape was late 1962 and it was made with twenty-seven other East Berliners through the newly dug Bernauer tunnel. It wasn't long afterwards that the tunnel filled up with water and became unusable. By this time, the Berlin Wall had just been up barely a year.

There wasn't always a wall or barrier but movement between East and West Berlin would be increasingly restricted as the years rolled on. Following lifting of the Soviet blockade in May 1949 the two regions of the city progressed at different rates with West Berlin outperforming its eastern counterparts, including basic standard of living. In October 1949, the German Democratic Republic (GDR) was formed from East Germany and the Soviet military occupation was stopped. Although, the Soviets still maintained a healthy presence in many East German institutions. So evident was this that in the early 1950s, many East Berliners wanted out, leading to a brain drain of educated and professional

## Part Three (1960-1966)

Germans. They left in droves: from 1949 to 1953, almost one million moved to West Berlin and ultimately West Germany. The year 1953 experienced particularly high migration due to Stalin's autocratic ways and his push for "sovietization" of East Germany. [81]

Young German citizens weren't the only ones building tunnels — the CIA eight years earlier had also entered the business. The Berlin Blockade and Stalin's moves in Europe had provided sufficient credence that communism was the new menace. The National Security Council, formed in 1947 had issued a directive jointly drafted by the State and Defense Departments titled NSC-68. The sixty-six-page report, in April 1950, had far reaching implications for America's preparedness and involvement in the Cold War. In fact, it guided government policy, military budgets and wartime participation for the next forty years. It was published three months prior to the Korean War.

NSC-68 stated that "the enemy should be weakened from within by an intensified campaign of covert economic, political and psychological warfare." Accordingly, it called for "the improvement and intensification of intelligence activities" to provide sufficient warning of a Soviet attack. By the time Eisenhower took office, he was clamoring for any shred of evidence as to Soviet war intentions and was frustrated by American intelligence service's failure to deliver. Churchill was said to have harbored similar dissatisfaction with Mi6 in Britain. Germany was considered the forefront of any new war and it was here that the most valuable source of Soviet intelligence was thought to be available. After the war, Berlin was where almost a hundred international telegraph and telephone lines crossed and by 1949, the Soviets had taken control of all trunk lines going in and out of East Germany. With the Soviet Union dropping the hydrogen bomb in August 1953, and the specter of nuclear war, an added sense of urgency took hold to better determine what their intentions were. [81]

In 1952, William (Bill) Harvey was assigned as base chief for West Berlin. His real mission was said to oversee the CIA's attempt to build a communications tunnel and a young Ted Shackley joins his staff the following year. Shackley became one of Harvey's standout agents and liaison contact with the British when it came to the tunnel. Harvey was a heavy drinker and an odd duck. With protruding eyes and a pear-shaped body, he's said to always carry a pearl handled pistol, even into restaurants. Belying his appearance, however, Harvey was known to be very shrewd and calculating. It was Harvey who was among the first to figure out that British Mi6 agent Kim Philby was a Soviet mole. It was also Bill Harvey who, in November 1961, headed up ZR/Rifle the agency's ultra-top-secret program to assassinate Fidel Castro. [97]

The process actually started with Walter O'Brien in 1952, even before Bill Harvey arrived. O 'Brien's job was to scout out potential areas to tap into Soviet communications with the focus on underground telephone cables. Reinhard Gehlen, the head of the BND, the German Federal Intelligence Service, however, soon alerted the CIA to the prime location of a crucial telephone junction, where three cables came together less than seven feet underground. It was also very close to the American sector. The proposed tunnel needed to be 1,800 feet long with two-thirds of it being under Soviet sector soil. Three thousand tons of soil also had to excavated and surreptitiously disposed of in one of the built warehouses having an extra deep basement. Fortunately, for the tunnelers, the water table was low in the area. [97]

The entire facility appeared as an innocuous radar site housing emergency response equipment so as to fool the Soviets and nearby residents. Not even the West German authorities were made aware of the project. The US dug a six-foot diameter tunnel using the Army Corps of Engineers, with a test tunnel first dug in New Mexico to test a roof bracing technique. The hole had to be big enough to accommodate various telecommunications equipment including signal amplifiers. The US paid for the tunneling and nearby buildings while the British supplied expertise and the means to tap into Soviet communication lines. A technique they had perfected previously by successfully tapping into Soviet lines in Vienna, doing so without a hint of voltage reduction. From start to finish the tunnel project would take about nine months to build, cost $6 million, and operate for eighteen months before it was discovered in April 1956 and shut down. [97]

## Part Three (1960-1966)

The joint US/British operation was called Operation Gold or PBJointly and it generated a vast amount of intelligence, much of it mundane but sometimes quite valuable. The immediate concern the allies had was that the Soviets would turn over the city to the East Germans sparking an international incident. The communications intercept indicated, however, that was not so and they intended to remain in control. Only in 1958, long after the tunnel was shut down, did Khruschev demand that Western forces withdrew from the city. Of course, they refused and that led to the building of the Berlin Wall in 1961. Other information obtained indicated the strength and positions of the Red Army and that the new Soviet T-52 tanks were prone to equipment failure. It also pinpointed locations that were involved in Soviet atomic research which the CIA and SIS previously weren't aware of. Finally revealed was that Khruschev's reforms following Stalin's death had actually strengthened Soviet nuclear capability, with new bombers and air bases being positioned in Poland. The Soviet's capability had grown stronger than previously thought but their intentions appeared more subdued... for the time being. [97]

In late 1963, twenty-one-year-old Joachim Neumann and a group of a dozen students set out to dig an escape tunnel the length of a football field. The digging with rudimentary tools took five months of grueling work, beginning at an abandoned bakery on the west side and ending inside an old outhouse behind an apartment building at Strelitzer Strasse 55. When opened, fifty-seven people were able to escape, including Neumann's girlfriend, Christa Ghrule who had been just released from prison for a prior escape attempt. After two days, the Stasi found out about the tunnel and closed it for good. Tunnel 57 was the last and largest mass tunnel escape to occur in Berlin. [81]

More than a hundred people died trying to escape from East Berlin prior to reunification, with another 250,00 detained simply for attempting flight or helping others to obtain a better life. Three hundred people, including Eveline Schmidt and her daughter, ultimately make it out.

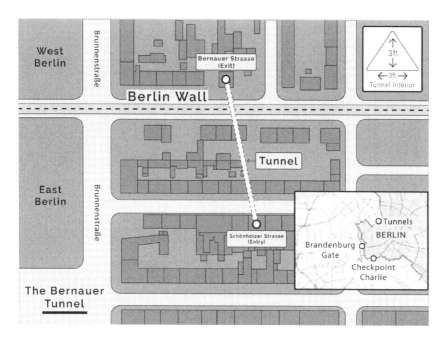

The Bernauer Tunnel (1962)

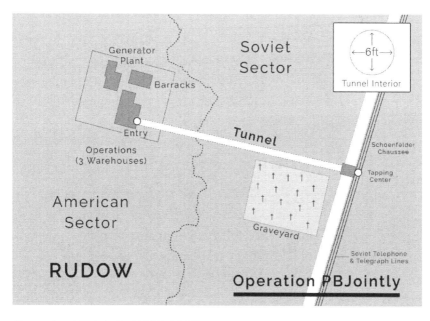

Operation PBJointly (1954-1956)

# Titans of the Plains

I moved to Colorado from Wiesbaden, West Germany in 1962, just as turbulent events were taking place in Berlin. In Wiesbaden, we lived in the fenced Hainerberg housing complex with other Americans. The most memorable experience was ever-present overcast skies during the two-year span while attending second and third grade. It was a time when Checkpoint Charlie would become a flashpoint between Soviet and American tanks and escapes from East Berlin a recurring norm. I had spent the first ten years of my life residing overseas, actually in the heart of Cold War Europe. Being raised in the land of my Norwegian mother's side of the family, it was now my father's turn to more fully Americanize me. Attending Montclair Elementary as a 4th grader in Denver, I remember pledging allegiance to my newfound country each morning before the ritual "duck and cover" drill common at the time. According to someone's infinite wisdom, my tiny wooden desk was believed to be able to withstand the mega-force impact of a thermonuclear blast. But those were the times then and the concern was not without merit. It was 1962 America, a tightly wrapped bundle of promise, fear and discord.

As a typical ten-year-old, I was preoccupied with exploring my neighborhood, keeping my grades up and deciding which girls would be getting my Valentine Day cards come February. World events rarely entered my consciousness nor as a kid would they have cause to. What I'd find out much later as an adult was that in the early 1950s, the nascent years of NATO, my airman father assigned to the US Embassy in Norway, had been approached one evening by a KGB agent. We were living in Oslo, Norway on Luftvartsvehen back then when one night, a

Soviet colonel struck up a friendly conversation, inviting my parents over to dinner with him and his wife. Not realizing who exactly he was talking to, my father grew suspicious and reported the incident to his superiors. Thus began a fourteen year "relationship" of regularly feeding innocuous documents for money, which of course was handed over to my father's superiors. It all ended with a final exchange in 1964 on the steps of Colorado's state capital. Obviously, not all spy and covert activities involve the CIA, but they also include just regular people, folks outside the typical clandestine norm.

At that time, I was somewhat ignorant of the fact that within a fifty-mile radius of Denver, there were eighteen active Titan ICBM missile silos. How close we were, in both history and proximity, to a possible Armageddon was a bit daunting. Frankly, how was a ten-year-old to even know? The Soviet Union had launched Sputnik in October 1957, heralding their prowess of launching and keeping a satellite in low earth orbit. That event, their later Tsar Bomba nuclear bomb test in 1961 and certainly the Cuban Missile Crisis, created public concern there was a "missile gap" between the Soviet Union and the United States. It was exacerbated also by the earlier Gaither Report which stated the US had been over-relying on its superior nuclear bomber force which it argued could be taken out by a Soviet sneak attack. The push was now on to not only create more powerful and reliable nuclear tipped missiles but also a lot more of them. [9, 42, 59]

The defense department had moved beyond the first-generation Atlas missiles to the larger, more powerful Titan having extended range and a bigger payload. They also wanted to relocate the ICBMs away from coastal regions, focusing instead on the central United States. As a result, construction overseen by the US Army Corps of Engineers began in May 1959 on six complexes that were housing three-missile silos, each. According to one source:

> "It was the largest and most expensive underground launch complexes ever built, and heavily hardened to survive a nuclear attack. They resembled underground futuristic cities with a half mile of tunnels buried more than forty feet underground." [91]

## Part Three (1960-1966)

Two assigned Air Force squadrons became fully operational by April 1962. The 724th Strategic Missile Squadron had the nearest three-silo complexes to the Denver metro area. In fact, two were only twenty miles away from Lowry Air Force Base where we were living. The 725th Squadron controlled the other three. The apparent objective for placing the missiles so close to Denver was to lessen the logistical burden placed on the contractor, nearby Martin Company (later Lockheed Martin). That October, all squadrons went to DEFCON 2, the second highest national alert category, in response to the on going Cuban Missile Crisis. The flat expanse of eastern Colorado was no more as eighteen Titans poked from their silos like ghostly fingers reaching out from the ground. A reduced alert status would be maintained on all of them until February 1965. [42, 59, 81]

The Titan I missiles were quite large, particularly in relation to later ICBMs. Over 100 feet in height and weighing 116 tons, they were America's first multi-stage intercontinental ballistic missile with a range up to 6,000 miles. The problem was they were propelled by RP-1, an enhanced kerosene then mixed with liquid oxygen. Fueling, a particularly fickle and dangerous procedure, took over 15 minutes while the missile was still underground, being then raised up using a giant elevator. With the time also necessary for the launch process meant an overall slow response time. Add to that, while the missile was above ground it was also vulnerable to enemy attack. The Titan I carried a W-38 nuclear warhead, having a 3.75 megaton yield. It wouldn't be until the Titan I was replaced with Titan II's that the warhead increased to 9 megatons, by carrying the W-53. A 9-megaton blast was said to level all structures within a 9 mile radius and cause lethal burns within a 20 mile radius. This, of course, is not to mention the deadly ionizing radiation. [81]

The W-53 was originally designed as a "bunker buster", made to destroy the deep, vast underground command complex at Chekhov/Sharapova, 42 miles south of Moscow. It's where the Soviet General Staff and Defense Council were known to be located during wartime. Some experts, including the CIA, later harbored doubts whether such underground destruction was even possible with the W-53. [56, 81]

The Russians weren't sitting around on their hands. After detonating the world's most powerful bomb, the 50 megaton Tsar Bomba, in October 1961, they continued working on their delivery systems. The Soviet R-36 missile began multi-year production in 1962 and was initially capable of carrying an 18-25 megaton warhead and having a 10,000-mile range. The R-36 could hit a US target in about 28 minutes following launch. The largest warhead in the Soviet arsenal at the time was the SS-18 which yielded a 25-megaton blast. [81]

It was clear the Soviets had a first strike advantage and that the Strategic Air Command (SAC) knew that. Nonetheless, in deploying the Titans, two of the six Titan missile squadrons were located on the Colorado Front Range close to Lowry AFB and in proximity to Denver, a major metropolitan area of close to a million people. If the Russians wanted to take out a third of our slow response Titans at one time, this was the perfect place to do it. That vulnerability may have been a reason why Operation Chrome Dome, putting nuclear bombs onboard continually airborne B-52s, was inaugurated. By June 1965, Defense Secretary McNamara came to reason and deactivated the Titan silos around Denver. A better solution of using ICBMs was be found with the next generation Titan II and Minuteman. The Titan II was retired in 1987, whereas the Minuteman III missiles are still very much in use today. [81]

## Part Three (1960-1966)

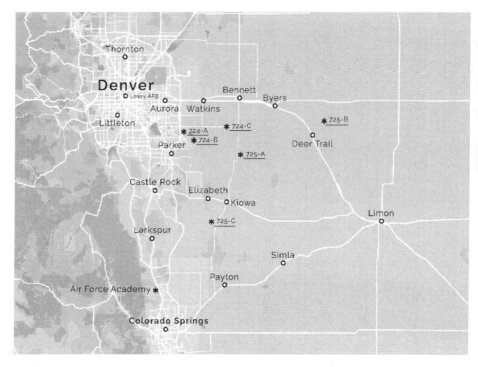

Denver, Colorado and Titan I Missile Silos (1960s)

# Finding Shangri-La

If Camp Hale was The Garden, then Long Cheng was Shangri-La. At least it was considered an idyllic spot by a number of people who first put eyes on it, including Vint Lawrence who called it "pristine and absolutely beautiful." It was also located just eighteen miles from Phou Bai, Laos' tallest peak standing majestically at over 9,000 feet. [52]

With an air of secrecy, exceeding even that of Tibetan training at Camp Hale, Long Cheng was considered for the longest time "The Most Secret Place in Earth." A valley nestled in the high Laos mountains surrounded by peaks and karst formations, it's about the most secluded place in Southeast Asia and high enough to produce chilly nights and a frequent cold fog. CIA agent Bill Young recommended the site to Bill Lair after the Hmong defeat at Pa Dong in June 1961, their primary training camp. Long Cheng (also known as Long Tieng) took over as the main Hmong camp until the end of the war. Beginning as a tiny hamlet with a corn patch nestled in a valley of wildflowers, it soon grew into a bustling city of 40,000 mostly Hmong inhabitants with no pavement or sewer system. By 1966, this secret location had one of the busiest airstrips in the world, yet it was not listed on any map. It would also no longer remain a secret from the North Vietnamese during the coming years. [23, 24]

Vint Lawrence, a 1960 art history major from Princeton, had already been drafted into the army when the CIA came to recruit him. Just twenty-two years old, he was chosen by Bill Lair to be the agency's advisor to Vang Pao. Knowing that Vang had a brutal side towards sworn enemies, Lawrence nonetheless bonded easily with him to the point Vang looked at him like a younger brother. This was partly due to Bill Lair instructions but mostly to Vint's own respectful manner. It was also likely something that likely grated on Tony Poe when they shared a thatched, dirt floor hut in Long Cheng the first few years. Poe wasn't always on the most cordial terms with Vang Pao as he was starting to build the rough edges he was later known for. [23, 24]

By now, Poe was 41 years old, balding and drinking and whoring like he'd just gotten out of boot camp. He also wasn't above an occasional bar fight, carrying around his boxing teeth guards and pair of brass knuckles. The male version of the biological clock for Tony Poe was ticking ever loudly. One day, near the flight line in Long Cheng, an attractive Hmong lady in slacks walked by, leading her young daughter.

> "Who is that? I need to meet her!" said Poe taking quick notice of her taut figure and shapely behind.
>
> "No, no, Vang Pao want to meet her," another Hmong replied. "She too tough. She just got rid of husband or he got rid of her.... something like that"
>
> "Oh, that woman. You don't want to know," said Vang Pao apparently overhearing the conversation. "She is danger." [38]

Knowing that Vang Pao also had his eyes on her made Tony Poe want her all that much more. Furthermore, he already had five or six wives. In due course, Poe did get to know the woman much better. She was Ly Sang, a niece of prominent Touby Lyfoung, Hmong political spokesman in Vientiane. French educated, Lyfoung, used to have the hilltribe heroin monopoly in the Plain of Jars, supplying product to the French Expeditionary Force. The French military were severely underfunded in an ever-unpopular war, despite receiving financial help from the US. Accordingly, Operation X was devised to funnel profits from Laos heroin in order to pay for covert operations and supply arms to ethnic tribes. During the early 1950s, Touby was joined by Lieutenant Vang Pao, a rising young Hmong company commander. Aside from the heroin business,

Lyfoung and Pao met periodically with French General Albert Sore providing him with intelligence and discussing paramilitary operations. A precursor, of sorts, to a similar arrangement Vang Pao later had with the CIA. [23, 24]

Ly and Poe did have something in common, both being nominal Catholics and Ly had received an early education from traveling missionaries. The marriage ceremony was held in March 1964 in Long Cheng, accompanied by a lot of chanting, beating drums and Poe still wearing his combat fatigues and .357 Magnum. Everyone attended, except Vang Pao, and given the respite from hostilities, the war seemed to have receded from consciousness for at least a day. Alluring Ly Sang would not come cheap for Tony Poe... her family's dowry amounted to a hundred water buffalo and seventy goats. [23, 38]

# Clash at Hong Nong

It was now January 1965, with Lyndon Johnson about to be inaugurated and the United States entering the thick of it in South Vietnam. It already had 23,000 military personnel on the ground later augmented by US Marines landing in March to guard Da Nang Air Base. The Marines would represent the first influx of American combat troops into the war. Under Operation Rolling Thunder, the US had also just commenced a three-year campaign of bombing selected targets in North Vietnam.

Vietnam was becoming a Cold War battleground with North Vietnamese and Pathet Lao the proxy soldiers for the Soviet Union and Chinese. The Soviets in 1965, recently had agreed to assist North Vietnam to defend itself from the Rolling Thunder air strikes, by providing surface-to-air missiles (SAMs), jet fighter planes, technical support and advisers. Just as in Korea, the Soviets preferred to remain in the background and simply provide the technology used in the conflict. To see how their latest advancements test out in a wartime laboratory particularly against what the Americans brought to bear including countermeasures they used. Taking a break from the nuclear race, the conflict in Southeast Asia would be an accelerated testing ground for conventional weapons technology between Cold War adversaries.

China's support no longer committed troops on the ground performing human wave attacks but rather provided the things the Soviet Union did not. Their support went back to the early 1950s when they provided small arms, mortars, ammunition and sent in advisors. After the Geneva Conference of 1954, that assistance was ramped up to also include Chinese anti-aircraft guns and food which became short in supply. Soldiers were also sent in and at its peak year in the mid 1960s, there were up to 170,000 Chinese troops operating in some capacity in North Vietnam. When the Chinese pulled back their assistance during the late 1960s, the slack was taken up by the Soviets.

In Laos, much of the early support was funneled through supplies provided by China to North Vietnam. The Soviet Union initially undertook a massive airlift in the fall of 1960, of equipment and supplies that was earmarked for Laos but transited through Hanoi. Since then, the Soviets toned down their commitment although much was still supplied indirectly via Eastern Bloc countries. Unlike China which shared a border with both Laos and North Vietnam, the Soviets didn't sense an immediate threat so preferred to remain one step removed from the ongoing conflict. The bulk of regular equipment coming directly into Laos arrived from China utilizing their new road network, extending into Laos from Yunnan Province. Monitoring Chinese road building became an early task for CIA operatives in northern Laos. [23]

During the early years, the North Vietnamese soldier was provided with a hodge podge of different weapons left over from World War II; however, by the early 1960s, most were using the Soviet-designed SKS carbine. It was lightweight and suited their needs quite well. By 1967, they exchanged their carbines for the AK-47, a heavier but more durable weapon firing the same ammunition but now included a thirty-round clip. They also used the K-50 submachine gun and different types of hand grenades, the most common being the Korean War relic potato masher. With deadly effect, the Soviet RPG-2 rocket propelled grenade was employed against armored fighting vehicles and fortified positions. It was known to penetrate sandbags up to six feet in depth. [35]

Probably the best weapon the North Vietnamese had was the soldier himself. Communist propaganda and political commissars painted the recurring picture that the people of South Vietnam were suffering under abuse and slavery and it was their moral duty to liberate them. They were told that America had "invaded" the south. Apparently, this line of thinking extended to assisting the Pathet Lao to liberate their country as well. [35]

## Part Three (1960-1966)

Like Vietnam, Laos was also far from quiet with the North Vietnamese actively moving convoys along Route 7 into the Plain of Jars. This major east-west arterial, originally built in the early 1900s was expanded during the French occupation. It was the chosen pathway for troops and supplies entering Laos from North Vietnam just as the Ho Chi Minh trail was for transporting materiel into South Vietnam. Despite Thai PARU's best attempts to blow up sections of the roadway, later assisted by aerial bombing, resilient Route 7 always found a way to stay relatively intact. [23, 24]

Conducting active reconnaissance in the general vicinity, Tony Poe had with him a small PARU team accompanied by Hmong fighters when a vicious firefight soon erupted. He had been warned previously by Bill Lair not to take part in actual fighting, however, he and his men were now being shot at and "damn if he was going to run away from a fight!"

"Help Me! HELP ME!

A cry for help went out, but Tony Poe could do nothing since a bullet had just ripped into his hip. He was on the ground and feeling nothing in his legs. [38]

"TONY, HELP ME!"

It was his Thai PARU team leader yelling. Poe had to block out the cries because he was in a life-or-death situation himself and needed to focus. He pulled four hand grenades off his harness and laid them out neatly onto the ground... all in a row and all within easy reach of his throwing arm. [38]

More Vietnamese were charging forward. Patiently waiting until they got close enough, Poe pulled the pin, counting 1-2-3 and let loose with his first grenade in a perfectly thrown arc. BOOM!! Muscle memory from his fighting days on Iwo Jima had now taken over.

He grabbed the next grenade... BOOM! Then the third one... BOOM! All perfectly choreographed in timing and motion. Poe was now down to his very last grenade, his last line of defense against a never-ending stream of

Vietnamese attackers. It was do or die time. He pulled out the pin, counted to three and lobbed his final grenade — BOOM! [38]

All of a sudden, everything was very still. Painfully, he pulled himself up to look around. Everyone was dead, bodies were lying all around, even his team leader who had been crying out for his help was dead. Tony Poe then glanced at his hip. It hurt like hell and was a bloody mess, even the bone was showing through. Using his M-1 rifle as a crutch, he managed to get up and hobbled back up to his command post.

Poe radioed the helicopter pilot flying high overhead saying he would be walking out, despite being wounded. He gave a location about five miles away where a chopper could land safely. So, off he struggled down one hill and across a creek to get there. He couldn't make it across the second hill so his Hmong fighters carried him while lying on a poncho. Nearing the landing site, the Thai soldiers accompanying him quickly skirted around to get onto the arriving helicopter. As they attempted to board, a thoroughly pissed off Tony Poe pointed his .357 Magnum at the three of them.... [38]

> "THIS CHOPPER IS FOR THE WOUNDED, GODDAMMIT!!" They apparently got the message and the helicopter took off with Poe and the onboard doctor but without the Thais. Poe informed the pilot to head back to where his wounded soldiers were.
>
> "The elevation is too high to carry so many passengers," protested the pilot.
>
> "Do it anyway!" Poe snapped back. "Doc, pull me over to the door so I can guide the pilot safely back to our command post." [38]

The waiting thirteen wounded Hmong were in pretty bad shape but all were successfully evacuated. Tony Poe, himself, was flown to the US hospital in Korat, Thailand where, in time, he recovered. He found out later that the helicopter's engine had completely burned out from the ordeal that day.

## Part Three (1960-1966)

Say what you will about Tony Poe — coarse, insubordinate, brutal, frequently a drunk — but that time was his finest hour. The true essence of the man was shown that day. While in recovery, Pat Landry popped in to check on him. Tony Poe, like many others, didn't particularly like Landry but he appreciated the gesture, nonetheless. After some perfunctory chit-chat, Landry showed Poe an article from a recent North Vietnamese newspaper proclaiming the heroic Pathet Lao had just killed an American advisor.

> "Look, you're dead!" said Landry, to which Poe replied,
> "Oh yeah? Well, that's good." [38]

It wouldn't be the first time Communist media jumped to claim a success or victory despite facts indicating otherwise. Tony Poe seemed satisfied with the final result, notwithstanding sustaining casualties and his own injury. The story quickly spread that Americans... well, actually one of them, cared for the Hmong and that would make a noticeable difference in morale when fighting their common enemy. Something that Poe had learned from his experience in the Marines was to put his men's welfare above his own. As he would later say, "You can be the biggest prick in the world, as long as you take care of your people." [38]

During this timeframe, Tom Fosmire, who had earlier been at Hua Hin in 1963, transferred up to Phitsanulok in northcentral Thailand when PARU and associated training began taking place there. Fosmire, while at "Pitts Camp", as it was commonly referred to, sustained a hard landing from a solo parachute jump, fracturing some of his vertebrae. Following recovery, he checked in on his buddy, injured Tony Poe, recuperating about an hour flight away. Tom Fosmire himself left the relative safety of Thailand and entered the ongoing fray that was Laos.

# It,s Zulu Time

"Much of prison life was composed of such trivial ritual. If it was not dictated to me, I imposed it on myself. In its observance, I could forget the larger facts of my existence, .. that I was serving a life sentence in a hostile land." [6]

- John T. Downey (prison -year 13)

The secret B-52 mission briefing began promptly at 18:00 in the Ready Room at U-Tapao Air Base, Thailand. The room was first secured and the crowd of mostly junior officers and crew were seated and instructed to synchronize their watches using a countdown linked to Zulu Time, "4-3-2-1-Sync".. Colonel Moore, the Airborne Commander, then started the briefing....

"The mission takeoff time for the first cell of three planes is 05:00 tomorrow" (a roll call was then made of each of the plane commanders in cell one). "The takeoff time for the second cell of three is 05:20" (another roll call is similarly made). As standard, aircraft in each cell maintained a 500-foot elevation distance from each other and one nautical mile laterally. Moore, using his pointer, referred to the big map pulled down behind him and continued...

"We will follow our usual Departure Route leaving U-Tapao, proceeding to Point A, then to Point B, to Point

C...." (at this stage in the war, all coordinate points were pre-determined to circumvent Cambodian and Laos airspace, while leading into the Saigon area). "At Point H, reduce altitude to 7,000 feet.

"Then head on to the Primary IP" (Initial Point is a pre-set coordinate over the Gulf of Tonkin, just north of Da Nang. After that point, the pilot had to fly straight and level with no evasive action taken in order to stabilize the bombing computer gyros). "Then proceed to the Primary Target at X26 (near Khe Sanh and the border) where there's a large enemy troop concentration and storage area.

"Open bomb bay 30 seconds prior to release on the primary target... after release, make a hard right turn (to avoid entering North Vietnamese airspace) and proceed to Alternate IP." Alternate Target (Pleiku in Central Highlands) followed Alternate IP and then return home to U-Tapao. There was a weather briefing by 1st Lieutenant Nichols followed at the end by an intelligence briefing by SSgt Lemon.

"Gentlemen, any questions?" as Colonel Moore asked, scanning the room. "Good luck."

The B-52 was initially conceived in October 1948, around the start of the Cold War. It followed production and use of the B-36 "Peacemaker" which was even larger with a wingspan of 230 feet compared to the B-52's 185 feet. Both planes were designed to deliver nuclear bombs yet, by 1955, the jet-engined B-52 would become America's chosen strategic bomber. [31, 60]

The D model, as used during Colonel Moore's mission in Vietnam, was known as "Big Belly", having been modified to also carry bombs externally. Pilots often say flying a B-52 takes a bit of strength... "It's like driving your grandfather's old cadilac." The crew of five officers included the pilot, co-pilot, navigator, radar-navigator (bombadier) and electronic warfare officer (EWO). There was also an enlisted man employed as tail gunner. A minute or so before bomb release, the plane's controls would be briefly turned over to the radar-navigator, ensuring precision delivery. The D models were all located at U-Tapao and could carry a conventional bomb load of 29 tons compared to only 16 for sorties leaving Andersen AFB, Guam. The latter planes would also require mid-air refueling due to their extended flight distance. [31]

There had been a continuing internal struggle within the Air Force from the early days over the role of strategic manned aircraft carrying nuclear bombs. The preeminence of intercontinental ballistic missiles over piloted bombers took place the late 1950s into the mid 1960s, culminating, in part, with the Cuban Missile Crisis. Within a few years, US defense's focus shifted as the Cold War heated into a traditional armed conflict in Southeast Asia. This was where the strategic B-52 bomber tested its mettle in conventional warfare, particularly in a real life setting where enemy combatants fired surface to air missiles. [31, 60]

The B-52 bombers had dominion over the skies during the early war years. It had an effective ceiling of 50,000 feet which was sufficient enough to avoid ground missiles until four Soviet SA-2 Surface to Air Missiles (SAMs) sites were deployed to North Vietnam in mid 1965. The SAM count quickly increased to 150 sites and air defenses were augmented by MiG-21s by year end 1966. From this point until the Cease-Fire Agreement in 1973, there'd be a continual cat & mouse game played between SAM radar operators and B-52 Electronic Warfare Officers with advances continually made in technology and improved tactics. As bombing intensity increased in the Hanoi and Haiphong area of North Vietnam in late 1972, under Operation Linebacker II, B-52 losses also increased. At the end of the war, the Strategic Air Command had 31 Stratofortresses lost from various wartime causes, with ten actually being shot down over enemy territory. By mid-1975, all remaining B-52s left U-Tapao for good. [60]

Lessons taken away from the Vietnam experience were that aircraft manufacturers simply couldn't build planes that go faster or higher in altitude hoping to escape ground launched missiles. A better way is to fly lower and make aircraft "stealthy", in other words, having an airframe that deflected or absorbed radar signals so little could be reflected back to the radar. By the mid-1970s, such technology was believed feasible so a heavy bomber's large signature would become nearly undetectable, at least by radar. Other methods such as infrared scanners and acoustic locators were still effective but they suffered from shortcomings, including having a shorter range. Developers saw the fruits of their labors in 1989 with the introduction of the B-2 bomber which could carry nuclear as well as conventional ordnance. [31]

# A Skyraider's Ordeal

It was a cloudless spring morning on the edge of Germany's Black Forest. He was holding his fiancé, Marina, so close from behind while smelling her hair-that radiant blonde hair. As she turned to face him, their eyes locked and a smile began to form. Supreme contentment and happiness overwhelmed him as he knew she was the one for him. Suddenly, her face began to fade and the blissful dream-state he was in quickly disappeared. He had rudely woken up to reality...

Dengler immediately felt stinging pain all over his head and neck. His face was burning and enflamed to the point of having trouble seeing out of his swollen eyes. He had been hanging upside down the entire night and had now been lowered nearly face down upon a colony of angry ants. His captors were laughing and talking animatedly about his helpless predicament. Not understanding what was being said, he knew, of course, who they were — they were communists, the Pathet Lao.

Just a few days before, Lieutenant J.G. Dieter Dengler was in his A-1 Skyraider on a mission over Laos. They'd just been informed January 1966 that the door was now open to bombing North Vietnam. But this was actually halfway into Laos, near Mu Gia Pass, a critical choke point and northernmost entrance to the Ho Chi Minh Trail. The target was a river crossing on Route 27 and any vehicles they were lucky enough to find enroute. With Dengler were four other Spads, the nickname given to propeller driven Skyraiders — a peculiar attack plane still lingering over from World War II during the present jet age. The squadron pilots, however, loved it. It could take multiple small arms hits, carried four 20 mm cannons, up to 8000 pounds of ordinance and could literally fly for hours.

## Part Three (1960-1966)

Actually, three to six hours compared to a jet's usual one and a half. These Spads were from VA-145 a squadron which called the USS Ranger home, lying just off Vietnam's coast near Da Nang. An earlier notable VA-145 wartime assignment had taken place back in 1958, during the Second Taiwan Crisis. [30]

The Mu Gia Pass mission had Ken Hassett listed as team leader, Malcolm "Spook" Johns, Denny Eastam followed by Dengler in the rear. The prescribed bombing formation was single file with Dengler coming in for the last drop as the thankless "tail end Charlie." This was a Korean War maneuver that Vietnam era pilots hated because by the time the last plane was making its bomb run, anti-aircraft gunners had already locked in on the planes. Despite flying 19 previous sorties, Dengler had a certain uneasy feeling about this mission. Before catapulting off Ranger's flight deck, he took one last glance at the small photo he kept of Marina in his cockpit.

They were over the target area within 40 minutes as the cloud cover began to break. The topography became noticeably different as Dengler looked upon a vast deep green jungle, punctuated by occasional rock outcroppings. *"Welcome to Laos,"* he thought. The other pilots quickly dropped their bomb loads and now it was Dengler's turn. No sooner had he released his, he was shocked by what he felt was a lightning bolt blasting up through the right wing, putting his plane into a spin. Then, as he managed to straighten out the plane, the engine suddenly cut out and wouldn't restart. He tried again to start it.... Nothing. [30]

> *"Oh shit! Do I bail out or stay in the cockpit?"* were the thoughts that raced through his mind.

The Spad had no ejection system. To bail out, the pilot had to toggle a switch which blew off the canopy, and he'd then stand up in the seat to jump out. If below 1,500 feet, forget it... it's too low to use a parachute. He blew off the canopy anyway.

"Damn it... I'll have to ride this out. I can do this," he kept reminding himself. It's known that the Spad stood a better chance of the pilot surviving a crash than a jet. It's much sturdier and could also land at slower speeds. Dengler buckled himself back into the seat and frantically looked for a suitable clearing in the seemingly endless sea of jungle. [30]

"Over there... There I found it!" The problem was that his now powerless plane was still speeding about 180 mph which was sixty mph too fast. The clearing, he estimated, was about 300-feet long. He urgently needed to slow down his rapidly descending Spad.

Spotting a lone tree near the middle of the clearing, he aimed for it, clipping off the damaged right wing near the fuselage which then caused his left wing to dip into the ground and also break off. The now wingless fuselage violently tumbled several times before coming to rest. Despite having gallons of fuel still aboard, there was no fire as Dengler had wisely thought of turning off the electrical systems at the last moment. Happy to be alive, although dazed and battered, he remembered he had to get away from the wreckage as fast as he could in case it did blow or if someone saw him coming down. Apparently, someone did and Dengler was quickly apprehended.

After the ant hill experience, Lieutenant Dengler was well into a prolonged jungle journey with his communist captors taking him who knows where. Many days and nights had passed and he soon lost track of time, at least days and dates. The Pathet Lao were pissed about his escape attempts. More so at his refusal to sign a proclamation condemning the United States. He had bamboo shards painfully inserted under his fingernails and into incisions made on his body. While savagely kicking and beating him with rifle butts, one man's rifle accidentally went off and shot a comrade in the stomach. Somehow Dengler was put to blame for that also. They finally got tired, leaving him curled up in a fetal position. He felt a swift kick to the back to ensure he received the last measure of their wrath. Soon, Dengler and his tormentors were back up again, trudging through the morass of steaming jungle, up and down the hills: day after endless day. [30]

After what appeared to be a fortnight, they approached a camp in a clearing near the village of Pa Kung. Apparently, it was a POW camp run by the North Vietnamese. The Vietnamese appeared a bit more polished than the ragtag

## Part Three (1960-1966)

Pathet Lao who were also present, although they could be just as brutal. In the camp, Dengler met fellow Americans Duane Martin, an Air Force First Lieutenant and rescue pilot and also Eugene DeBruin. DeBruin and three Thai prisoners had been civilian cargo kickers for Air America. One of the Thai had been a Royal Thailand Army paratrooper (PARU) before he changed to pushing payloads out the back of C-46s. They'd all been imprisoned at several POW camps for up to two and half years and like them, he too had his ankles secured in wood blocks every night. Dengler was simply astounded at the length of their incarceration. As he later recounted:

> "The years were etched on their faces, and in their sunken, haunted eyes there was a sadness that could not be hidden by their brief smiles and friendly greetings to me. They would each ask, 'Is the war winding down? How is the Geneva Peace Talks coming? Is there any word on a prisoner exchange?'"
> [30]

Dengler knew he couldn't lie to these men. They lived on hope but it shouldn't be a false hope. After all this was still 1966, during President Johnson's escalation of the Vietnam war — certainly a long way off from the end and dealing with such things as prisoner exchanges. Maybe their perception of time became altered while imprisoned or maybe it was simply hope fueling their will to live. He convinced them that escape really was the best option; in fact, it was the only option. Certainly that was now forefront in Dengler's mind and detailed plans were soon formulated for the coming monsoon season. The danger, as these men reminded him, was the jungle and its lack of drinking water, not so much the prison camp. The rural Pathet Lao were shown to be adept at monitoring most of the water holes. Monsoon rains would level that playing field but they were still many months away from the wet season. Time would pass, boredom occasioned by periodic brutality and captured rats providing the necessary protein to their abysmal diet.

On many a morning, as Dengler watched early streams of sunlight dance across his earthen floor, his mind would drift off to Marina. He really wanted her to visit his native Germany, his quaint little village of Wildberg nestled in the Black Forest region. Dengler had grown up in post-war Germany when times for his family were tough. Being so young, he didn't recall much of the war itself but remembered what the Soviets did in partitioning his country, the Berlin Wall and the American led airlift that kept Berliner's alive. There were good reasons why Germans preferred a surrender to Americans than capitulating to the Russians. He loathed communism with its distortion and abuse by autocratic rulers, essentially being no better than Hitler's Nazis. Dengler liked Americans much more and he came to his adoptive country to learn to fly, and to fight for it. Yes, he longed for Marina to see his birth country as it was at that present time. But first, he had to get out of this hell hole... [30]

Torrential rains finally came, and a prison break was made using separate small teams. Of all the escapees, only Dengler and a Thai man were known to have ultimately succeeded. Dengler had initially teamed up with Duane Martin and apparently they'd been walking around in circles for several weeks since leaving the camp. Martin, the physically weaker of the two, would be killed in a machete attack by a rural villager. Dengler was now entirely on his own.

Then one day, Dengler, alone in a riverbed, was spotted frantically waving next to an SOS sign he'd written on a rock. A Spad passing overhead took notice and radioed for a Search and Rescue (SAR) helicopter. Air Force SAR pilot of the MH-53 "Jolly Green Giant" flying out of Quang Tri was none other than Captain William Cowell. Cowell, previously assigned to the air base at Udorn, Thailand had piloted the helicopter that checked out Dengler's crash site six months earlier... a hundred miles away. He was just one day too late. [30]

When doctors examined an emaciated Dengler, he was found to have intestinal worms, fungus, jaundice, hepatitis and two forms of malaria. He weighed only 95 pounds. Doctors told the rescue pilots if they hadn't found him when they, did he would have likely died in a day or two from severe malnutrition. A relieved Dengler was allowed to send a quick message to Marina ....

**Part Three (1960-1966)**

> "I ESCAPED FROM PRISON. ALIVE IN HOSPITAL. WILL
> BE HOME SOON. LOVE YOU. [30]
> - DIETER."

On October 7, 1966, Dieter Dengler, following months of recovery, was discharged from San Diego Naval hospital. A day later, he married Marina Adamich in Reno, Nevada. [30]

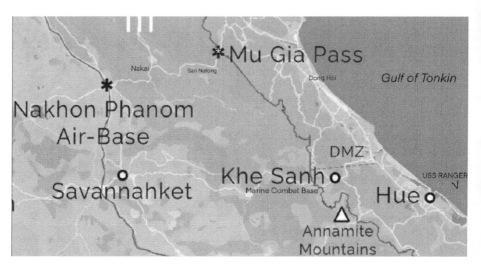

Mu Gia Pass (1966)

# Duty in Savannakhet

"In the early years in prison, I had longed for companionship. Fecteau and I had begged to share a cell. But in my last years, I cherished my isolation. I knew I could outwait my captors, and I didn't need the depressions and fears of some strangers. The tedious burdens and daily indignities of prison life were better borne by me alone." [6]

- John T. Downey (prison -year 14)

Tom Fosmire became the CIA man in charge of Military Region 3 (MR-3) in 1966 and remained in that position for three years. MR-3 is at the upper end of the Laos panhandle in Central Laos, encompassing Khammouan and Laos' largest province, Savannakhet. Fosmire was based in the town of the same name. He had three Continental Air Services Pilatus Porter planes and two Air American UH-34 helicopters at his disposal, all flown by Thai air crews. One hundred and fifty miles south was Pakse, which oversaw military Region 4 (MR-4) whereas just sixty miles north right across the Mekong in Thailand was Nakhon Phanom which saw the Navy Seabees in 1962 build a runway and other facilities at the Thai air base. The Air Force's Air Rescue squadron and Air Commando Wing later relocated there as would Special Forces elements and Air America. Air Force jets and bombers conducted their operations out of other Thailand bases. Fosmire and his staff had an important mission, to monitor what was transpiring on the Ho Chi Minh Road, little more than a hundred miles due east. [34]

## Part Three (1960-1966)

These were the Road Watcher Teams operating out of Savannahket, conducting photo reconnaissance. They found that the North Vietnamese had installed a pipeline to fuel their vehicles along the route. Previously, one fuel truck would have had to accompany three transport trucks and before that, fuel was hand carried by porters. Gasoline, diesel and kerosene ran through the plastic line with periodic pump stations set up along the way. Bill Lair had his doubts, so Fosmire had his people cut a 3-foot section of the 4 inch pipe which Fosmire personally brought to Lair's office in Udon Thani, placing it on his desk. The North Vietnamese were amazingly adaptable with not only expanding the reach of the trail but making it more efficient and safer from airborne interdiction. [34, 38]

Little did Fosmire first realize that there were many Pathet Lao run prisoner camps in the region owing to the importance of the Ho Chi Minh Trail and proliferation of flyers wanting to photograph or interdict it. His office had been getting reports of sightings of enemy camps which included three captured Americans, maybe more. Details were sorely lacking and it seems the Pathet Lao would keep constantly on the move, taking prisoners from one location to the next. In a year's time, a Pathet Lao defector provided the details necessary, including a count of about forty prisoners. After his interrogation, the defector agreed to accompany a rescue team which was put together. A Sergeant Te assembled a select rescue team of ten capable Lao soldiers of his choosing, calling it Team Cobra. Arriving at the POW camp, they found there were twice as many prisoners, but unfortunately, no Americans.

One of the prisoners, however, was Phisit Intharathat, a Thai who had been working for Air America. His C-46 was shot down in September 1963 with Gene DeBruin, an Air America cargo kicker. A couple years later in December 1965, 1st Lt Duane Martin was brought into Phisit's camp. Tall, handsome but looking very weak and badly bruised, Martin appeared happy to see Debruin, a fellow American. He related his story of having been shot down in his chopper while trying to rescue a downed F-5 pilot. In May 1966, the prisoners made the acquaintance of recently captured Navy Lieutenant Dieter Dengler at a new prison called Ban Hoeui Het. Dengler and Martin later made an escape together with only Dengler surviving. Dengler told his story from his own perspective in the chapter titled, "A Skyraider's Ordeal." [34, 38]

Phisit and many others, but not all, were rescued by Sgt Te's men as there were found to be more than 80 prisoners at the camp. Phisit later met Tom Fosmire, the CIA agent setting the whole rescue raid in motion, recognizing him as his radio instructor back when he first joined Air America. The Ban Naden Raid of January 9, 1967 went down as the only successful rescue of POWs during the VIetnam War. Tom Fosmire hadn't informed his superiors at Udorn of the mission until after it was completed, as he believed they might jeopardize it. No Americans, including Gene DeBruin, were among those rescued that day. The Pathet Lao decades later stated that DeBruin had been killed following an escape attempt. Others including Thai and Lao residents as well is an American POW organization contend DeBruin had been living with his Lao wife and family in nearby Khamouane Province.

The years 1966 to 1968 brought about a dramatic escalation to the Vietnam conflict and associated activity going on in Laos. The old guard of Vint Lawrence, Bill Lair, Pat Landry in Laos were on their way out or marking their 'short time' calendars. Tom Fosmire left for duty in Vietnam just as Ambassador Sullivan passed the torch to fellow diplomat, George Godley. Importantly, 1966-68 marked the period that Ted Shackley took over as CIA Station Chief in Laos. [34, 38]

By the time Tony Poe was released for duty following recuperation from his injuries, Vint Lawrence was on the way out. Young Vint had taken charge of running Long Cheng and made numerous improvements like building a new airstrip, leveling out the valley floor to accommodate better habitations and grading a road route between the base and Sam Thong. Sam Thong was where USAID ran their operations under Edgar "Pop" Buell supplying food and sundries to the Hmong. Grumpy and complaining Tony Poe was back in old form and in no time was squabbling again with Vang Pao. Vang had been promoted to Major General in the Royal Lao Army and was in charge of the military region. That standing, however, didn't prevent Poe from criticizing Vang for trying to buy houses for his wives in Vientiane and commandeering Air America flights for his wives' junkets. Irritably, Tony Poe did have a valid point.

In relative short order, Bill Lair packed off Poe to the quietest military region in Laos, the far northwest. A sector, however, having its own set of issues for Poe to deal with. While things quieted down for Poe they heated up for other areas of Laos when the "new sheriff in town", Ted Shackley, arrived. Shackley said he was there to make the war in Laos bigger and more modern. While matters were proceeding relatively well in the northern Laos, it was struggling in the south, particularly when it came to preventing the flow of supplies coming down the Ho Chi Minh trail. [34, 38]

This was no longer a war for Lao's independence that was kept deliberately small and manageable; instead, it was now a conflict serving America's greater need in Vietnam. Sullen, pale, tall, and ambitious, Shackley was the CIA's chosen one to ramp things up. The logical choice for station chief would have been Lair but the agency liked Shackley's diverse experience of serving in Berlin and later in Miami, during the Cuban Missile Crisis. Furthermore, the CIA had a bias against agents residing too long in one post or area. Lair had been in Thailand and Laos now for sixteen years, married a Thai woman connected to the royalty and had essentially "gone native." [51]

The focus was clearly on Vietnam now where US troop levels had risen to 385,000 the year Ted Shackley came aboard. Under Shackley, new intelligence facilities were built at Udorn air base, the number of agency employees increased dramatically and air support also increased. He also brought many of his own team in from Miami. Tom Fosmire was still retained in Savannahket but the CIA man in Pakse was replaced by Dave Morales, whose strategy of using indigenous people as strike forces began having a detrimental effect. [39]

# Operation Chrome Dome

It was the "summer of '66." No, not the bestseller from Dan Wheatcroft or song by Gawen Robinson of the same name, but rather a chapter taken from the story of my own life. In mid-1966, my father, by now a senior Air Force NCO, was transferred from Denver to Torrejon AFB outside Madrid. One of the things I remember foremost is the fascist Francisco Franco's La Guardia Civil patrolling our housing complex wearing their odd looking "tricornio" hats and toting submachine guns. Franco was someone Eisenhower felt he could deal with which led to the Pact of Madrid in 1953 and three US air bases and a naval base built on Spanish soil. Little would I realize then, as a 13-year-old looking forward to three years of living in historically rich Spain, that critical events had already been in play just months before. Events that could have produced catastrophic consequences.

In January 1966, a B-52G laden with four B28F1 thermonuclear hydrogen bombs crashed mid-air with a KC-135 tanker while refueling. One bomb alone that was 1,000 times more powerful than dropped on Hiroshima; it was a blast that could easily level a major European City. The B-52G had transited the expanse of the Atlantic, after taking off from Seymour Johnson AFB in North Carolina. The flight plan called for the plane's lengthy mission to proceed through the Mediterranean to the Soviet European border and then to return. In the morning of 17th of January, the second of two refuelings took place at 31,000 feet with a KC-135 flying out of Moron AFB near Seville in southern Spain. As the B-52G pilot Major Larry Messinger later recalled:

> "We came in behind the tanker, and were a little bit fast, and we started to overrun him a little bit. There is

a procedure they have in refueling where if the boom operator feels that you're getting too close and it's a dangerous situation, he will call out, 'Break Away, Break Away! 'However, there was no call for a break away, so we didn't see anything dangerous about the situation. - but then all of a sudden... ALL HELL BROKE LOOSE!" [58, 81]

The planes collided with the refueling boom first striking the B-52G fuselage and snapping off the left wing, resulting in a major explosion. All four crew aboard the tanker were killed and four of the seven onboard the B-52G as well. Three of the four nuclear bombs were dropped out over land in the Palomares vicinity. In two of them, the conventional explosives exploded spreading radioactive contamination over residential and farm areas which fortunately was contained but required extensive cleanup. Air Force nuclear first responders initially buried the radioactive soil in trenches but later that soil would be removed to the US for proper disposal. Traces of contamination were still being found in the area up to forty years later. While there's been no reports of health issues involving Palomares residents, a marked increase was noted in long term cancers amongst the first responder group.

Three thermonuclear bombs were found but the fourth one was still missing. Following a major US Navy search, it was finally located at the bottom of the sea two months later but was dropped again during the recovery attempt. Located now at a depth of almost 3,000 feet, the bomb was successfully retrieved by a US Navy Deep Submergence vehicle in April 1966, just months before my arrival in Spain. Benidorm, a favorite beach town our family enjoyed every summer, was just 150 miles up the coast from the Palomares crash site. In March 2009, Time Magazine would comment that the Palomares incident was "One of the world's worst nuclear disasters." It easily could have turned out much worse. [58, 81]

Torrejon, up to April 1966, had been a Strategic Air Command base hosting SAC's 3970th Strategic Air Wing and also Operation Reflex. Under Reflex, B-47 Stratojets were staged at various select bases as additional nuclear force projection. They couldn't remain in the air nearly as long as B-52s, so their deterrent value relied on expanding the geographic scope of airborne B-52s by assignment to bases within proximity to the Soviet Union. Torrejon, interestingly, reverted from strategic to a tactical focus with hosting fighter squadrons and terminating Reflex operations the same time as the fourth nuclear bomb was found. Neither the B-52 nor the K-135 that crashed were assigned to Torrejon but the base took overall control of the search and the resulting political fallout. Spain did not allow B-52s to be flown in their airspace again until 1983.

Chrome Dome is the brainchild program started in 1961 by General Thomas Power of the Strategic Air Command. It happened about the same time that Titan I missiles were deployed in silos east of the Denver metro area. His thinking was that armed bombers already in the air would ensure the US had a second-strike opportunity should the Soviets decide to take out the SAC bases. At any one time, twelve B-52 nuclear laden bombers would be aloft, flying one of two routes with each mission lasting about 24 hours. One route took a B-52 up around the arctic region of Canada with airborne refueling conducted over Alaska. The other route followed that taken by Major Messinger during Palomares' incident. [58, 81]

General Power certainly didn't want Operation Chrome Dome to be kept secret including the fact the crew had the all the necessary codes and procedures to activate and arm the bombs. It's deterrence value lie in the Soviets 'knowledge that this was happening and to behave accordingly. In fact, SAC increased the airborne flights to 75 per day during the height of the Cuban Missile Crisis. Premier Nikita Khrushchev later wrote with a measure of grudging respect:

> "About 20 percent of all US Strategic Air Command planes, carrying atomic and hydrogen bombs, were kept aloft around the clock." [58]

The program wasn't without its problems, being preceded by a deplorable accident rate. During the 1950s, there were many nuclear accidents involving planes whether the bombs were armed or not. They were typically less serious and usually involved B-29s, B-36s and B-47s before the B-52s took over in 1961. Beginning that year, three serious mishaps would occur before Palomares. The one afterward took place in January 1968 on the northern Canada route and was caused by a seemingly benign event... placing an extra seat cushion too close to a heat source. Smoke from the resulting fire overwhelmed the crew's efforts to extinguish the fire, so they bailed out near Thule AFB in northern Greenland. Six of the seven crew members survived but four thermonuclear bombs had spilled out into frigid Arctic waters and were never found. Scattered plane wreckage and radioactive debris required extensive cleanup with plutonium and tritium being deeply imbedded in the ice. [58, 81]

On the morning of the crash, the Strategic Air Command felt it had enough and decided to shut down Chrome Dome for good. The program probably lasted two or three years longer than it should have. Titan II and Minuteman intercontinental missiles by then had replaced the Titan I and proved to be a more effective and safer deterrent. The Navy had also entered the picture with the Polaris and later Poseidon missiles, using submarines as a hidden mobile launch platform. The B-52 bombers continued their role as our nuclear mainstay but would now relegate their alert readiness to the ground. [58]

Palomares, Spain (1966)

# PART FOUR (1966-1976)

# The Great Purge

"The Chinese Communist Party was officially atheistic, but in its early years it was more tolerant toward religion than its Soviet counterpart. For years I heard the cathedral bells ring out each Sunday. They were finally silenced during the Cultural Revolution." [6]

- John T. Downey (prison -year 16)

Launching the Cultural Revolution in May 1966, Chairman Mao charged that bourgeois elements had infiltrated the government and society with their implied goal of restoring capitalism. Mao's wife Jiang Qing, Lin Bao and Zhou Enlai were also members of the inner circle he selected to stamp out negative cultural influences while also bolstering Mao's cult image. Lin Bao, who had been one of Mao's generals during the siege of Changchun in 1948, was credited with inventing Mao's Little Red Book. Everyone was given the book and required to carry it on their person, prepared to recite its slogans at public events. Mao badges and posters were made up by the millions and began appearing everywhere. Entertainment now was restricted to Mao Thought Propaganda Teams singing Mao's quotations set to music, while enthusiastically waving the Little Red Book. [1]

The first target for this government sponsored terror were the schools and universities. Students, being young and somewhat malleable, were told to denounce their teachers and administrators for "poisoning their heads with bourgeois ideas." Numerous student groups formed together calling themselves the "Red Guards." Almost immediately, violence erupted with teachers being dragged out, beaten and humiliated in public. Mao's exhortations ratcheted up the violence even further with Red Guard groups soon appearing everywhere. A mob-like mentality quickly spread out all across China. At a later point, when things were obviously getting out of hand, Mao instructed Enlai to publicize "Denounce by words, not by violence" which allowed some Red Guards to opt out of the brutality. But the violence continued anyway.

> "At the Peking Girls School, the headmistress was the first known death by torture that took place. The headmistress, a fifty-year-old mother of four, was kicked and trampled by the girls, and boiling water was poured over her. She was ordered to carry heavy bricks back and forth; as she stumbled past, she was thrashed with leather army belts with brass buckles, and with wooden sticks studded with nails. She soon collapsed and died. Afterwards, leading activists reported to the new authority. They weren't told to stop... which really meant to carry on." [1]

On August 18, 1966, dressed in army uniform for the first time since 1949, Mao stood on Tiananmen Gate to review hundreds of thousands of Red Guards. This was when the Red Guards were first introduced to the world. A leading perpetrator of the atrocities at the Peking Girl's School where the headmistress was killed had been given the honor of putting a Red Guard armband on Mao. [1]

Lao She was one of China's best-known writers. The 69-year-old was lauded by the Communist regime as "the people's artist." He was one of thirty of the country's leading writers, opera singers and other artists who were made to kneel in front of the bonfire and were all set upon again with kicks, punches, sticks and brass-buckled belts. The following day, Lao She committed suicide by drowning himself in a lake. [1]

One of Mao's objectives was to use the Red Guards like proxy bandits. They also confiscated tons of gold, silver, platinum, jewelry, and millions of dollars in hard currency, which all went into the state coffers, as well as many priceless antiques, paintings and ancient books. The top Communist leaders were allowed to take their pick of the booty. Mao's wife selected an 18-carat gold French pendant watch, studded with pearls and diamonds, for which she paid a paltry seven yuan, about one dollar. Mao, an avid reader, is known to have pilfered thousands of valuable books. [1]

Mao, unlike Stalin, made sure that much of the violence and humiliation in China was carried out in public view, with perpetrators often being direct subordinates of their victims. Photographing and filming denunciation rallies and foes being tortured also became a common practice with Mao enjoying looking at past recordings. [1, 81]

The outlying provinces suffered greatly. One of the worst-ravaged provinces was Inner Mongolia, where Mao harbored suspicions about a plot to detach the province and link it up with Outer Mongolia."Post-Mao official figures revealed that over 346,000 people were condemned and 16,222 died as a result of just one case. The number of people in the province who "suffered" in some way was later officially put at over one million... of whom 75 percent were ethnic Mongols. [1]

Another province that went through great trauma was Yunnan, in the southwest, where (according to official figures) in one trumped-up case alone, nearly 1,400,000 people were persecuted under the new provincial boss, General Tan Fu-ren. Seventeen thousand of them were either executed, beaten to death, or driven to suicide.

In 1965, a year before the Cultural Revolution began, China had created the Tibet Autonomous Region which now included only half of the territory prior to the invasion. The remainder was incorporated into four existing southwestern

# The Great Purge is not in body... 

Chinese provinces. During the Cultural Revolution, China imprisoned thousands of monks and nuns, burned sacred texts and destroyed all but eleven of Tibet's 6,200 monasteries in an attempt to wipe out Tibetan culture and religion. By the late 1970s, 1.2 million Tibetans had died as a result of the occupation. [1]

One brave 19-year-old university student wrote the following letter to Mao after witnessing his rally of the Red Guards at Tiananmen Square:

> "Dear Chairman Mao Zedong,
>
> The Cultural Revolution is no mass movement. It simply consists of a single man holding a gun to the heads of the people. What are you doing? Where are you leading this country? As a member of the Communist Party, please think about what you are doing."
>
> - She ended the letter by resigning from the Communist Party's Youth League [1]

Wang Rongfen then bought and drank a bottle of insecticide outside the Soviet Embassy. She had hoped the Russians would find her body and publicize her protest to the world. Instead, she woke up in a police hospital. Wang was sentenced to life in prison for her impertinence. Eventually, after twelve years, she was released in 1979 when Deng Xiaoping sought to undo many of the injustices committed under previous leaders. [1, 81]

In the ten years from when Mao started the Purge until his death in 1976, at least three million people in total died from violent deaths. Chinese leaders coming after Mao have acknowledged that a hundred million people or one-ninth of the entire population, suffered in some manner during the Cultural Revolution. The killings were largely known to be orchestrated by the state, with only a small percentage actually being at the hands of the Red Guards. It was really a mass purge of perceived threats against Mao Tse-tung, himself, more so than a cleansing of society. Given that the Chinese lost 180,000 killed during the Korean War, it seemed their worst enemy was their very own government. [81]

## Part Four (1966-1976)

What Mao failed to grasp was that by severely purging his people, schools and government, he was depriving China of the capacity for technological advancement which he so desperately sought. He was still relying on outside sources, such as the Soviet Union for his Superpower Program, which was still continuing. The disparity in armament advancement alone became crucially apparent in 1969 when China came to blows with the Russians over a border dispute. In the western region of Xinjiang, Mao was in awe of the Soviet tanks and artillery crossing the border. Russian air power and even its logistical network were superior to what the Chinese had, not to mention the nuclear disparity. Radical house cleaning during the Cultural Revolution instilled a pervasive climate of fear which shut down creative thinking, risk taking and innovation — factors considered necessary to pull China out of its pre-industrial state. Aside from simply being morally reprehensible, the purge defied common logic and reason why such a mandate was even put into motion and then allowed to continue for so long. The Maoist system and unchecked cult building of its totalitarian leader allowed it to happen.

# Raid on Phou Pha Thi

John Daniel was about finished unloading cargo from the Air America resupply chopper when an unusual noise caused him to look up. He was astounded by what he saw. Two North Vietnamese bi-planes were about to attack their mountaintop radar site.

> "WHAT!? I really didn't know what the hell it was," said Daniel who felt it looked like a scene right out of a World War I movie. [53]

But these aircraft, while bi-planes, were equipped for creating havoc. They were Antonov AN-2 Colts more recently made in the USSR. While prized for their adaptability, minimal landing requirements and slower speed, they were probably best suited for reconnaissance-type missions. The North Vietnamese, however, mounted 57mm rockets under the wings and a hole was made in the floor where 120mm mortar rounds could be slid down a tube to be dropped on targets. These garage shop versions of a modern-day bomber carried a top speed of 160 mph. [83]

Stan Sliz was watching the unusual sight along with a Thai captain who took a shot at an approaching plane with his rifle. The round hit the plane just as the pilot released his two rockets, causing the plane to jerk upwards and the rockets to pass harmlessly overhead. More salvos of rockets were followed by mortar from both planes. The rockets missed the radar building and the mortars were largely ineffective. It was good fortune, considering the radar site never thought about an attack from the skies and had no anti-aircraft guns to speak of. Pilots

## Part Four (1966-1976)

Ted Moore and Glenn Woods jumped into their undamaged UH-1 Huey helicopter and gave chase to the planes. At the last moment, Woods grabbed an available AK-47 rifle, thinking it would come in handy.

One plane was only going 120 mph, probably being the one that was hit by the Thai captain. The Huey, with a top speed of 135 mph and being more maneuverable, soon overtook the slower plane. Now looking downwards upon the plane, Woods carefully leaned out the Huey's open door and let loose a burst of gunfire from his AK-47 into the bi-plane's cockpit. Moore and Woods looked on in amazement at what they had just done as the plane slowed and crashed into the nearby hillside. [83]

Thinking if they could do it once, they could certainly do it again, Moore and Woods gave chase to the second bi-plane. A more confident Moore got in close to the second plane while Woods let loose with his rifle again, aiming once more at the unprotected pilot and not the plane itself. It ended up crashing about three miles away from the first one. Two other AN-2 Colts, which had been monitoring the unfolding action from a distance, quickly beat a retreat back to North Vietnam.

Four Hmong, including two women, were killed in the bi-plane attack in January 1968 but the radar came out unscathed and operations quickly resumed. This incident of a helicopter having shot down not one but two planes is considered a first in aerial combat history. The American embassy in Vientiane promptly sent a cable to Washington mentioning the aerial attack, ending with the following note:

> "We do not believe this incident necessarily introduces
> a new dimension to the war in Laos." [83]

Life reverted to a semblance of normalcy after the attack. Maybe the North Vietnamese thought the mile high massif, known as Phou Pha Thi, with a 3,000 foot near vertical drop on three sides was simply too tough to conquer. The base itself was guarded by 1,000 Hmong warriors. Maybe it was simply better for them to just go around it, focusing their resources on already planned operations further west.

Normal for a typical crew meant manning the radar site with two weeks onsite and a couple spent down on Udon Thani Air Base. While perched at the Lima Site's "eagle nest", they'd break into two 12-hour shifts, manning the radar equipment. The off-duty men slept in bunk beds in the nearby living quarters building, while the active shift manned the modern radar equipment. "State of the art" was a more appropriate phrase to use for the MSQ-77 which guided aircraft to the precise point in the sky where bombs were to be released. It also worked in tandem with the AWACS planes continually circling above the Gulf of Tonkin. [83]

The Air Force, by 1967, had several of these MSQ-77's in operation in South Vietnam and one even in Thailand. However, the one at Lima Site-85 was the only one reaching far into North Vietnam, requiring an unobstructed range of up to 175 miles away. Importantly, the MSQ-77 was just as effective in bad weather as it was in good conditions. Essentially giving no reprieve to Hanoi, which previously counted on regrouping during the bombing break provided by monsoon season. Now there was no break so that President Johnson could apply maximum pressure on the North Vietnamese, inducing them to enter peace talks. It actually had just the opposite effect. The North Vietnamese applied their own pressure to wear down the US government and public sentiment for the war. They launched the countrywide TET Offensive in January 1968, just about the same time the bi-planes paid a visit. A couple months later…

> "Hey guys, how do you want your steaks?" asked John Daniel, self-appointed barbecue chef having already finished his own shift at 6pm. About five men were standing around chit chatting, anxiously waiting for dinner. [53]

Bill Blanton, suddenly rushed over after being informed by the CIA guys of an eminent enemy attack. He, like all the others, were "sheep dipped" Air Force officers and noncoms. Because they were in supposedly "neutral" Laos they all took on the look and credentials as civilian Lockheed employees. In reality, Blanton was a Lieutenant Colonel as well as being the group's deputy commander. He quickly gathered 15 men together.... [83]

> "Men, we have a problem," he said after having radioed his boss in Udon Thani. "We opted to stay overnight and do tonight's missions as we planned. Hopefully, we'll get the choppers here in the morning."
>
> Just when everyone nodded their agreement with his plan, BOOOM!! [53, 83]

A rocket round landed right at Daniel's barbecue grill. Had the men standing there earlier not gathered around Blanton, they would have all been instantly killed. No more rockets were subsequently launched and things became quiet enough for the men to slip into their sleeping bags around midnight. Little did they realize that North Vietnamese commandos had been scaling the steep west mountainside the past few hours, the very same rock face everyone thought was unscalable. The rocket barrage started up again around 3:30am, waking everyone up. [83]

Then the barrage suddenly stopped, when the commandos had reached the summit and split up. One group was ordered to prevent nearby Thai soldiers from rushing to the rescue. The others entered the MSQ-77 radar building and killed most of the occupants, including Blanton. Richard Etchberger and several others, including Daniels and Sliz, sought refuge on a nearby lower rock edge which contained a small alcove. The commandos found them and started lobbing grenades down onto the group, killing two of them.

> "All hell was breaking loose," said Stan Sliz who, in his military life, was an Air Force captain. [53, 83]

When the grenades landed near them, the men tried to throw many right back or tossed them over the cliff. Hank Gish was killed early on so his body was quickly rolled over to absorb a blast clearly meant for Stan Sliz. Sliz was rendered semi-conscious and remembered talking to God and recalling promises he made to his wife that he'd make it back to her. When he regained consciousness, he overheard Etchberger and Daniel discussing their limited options, including surrendering. [83]

> "That's bullshit! Those fuckers aren't taking any prisoners!" Sliz said angrily. They all agreed with him. [53]

Daniel and Etchberger then radioed to call in air strikes on their position, asking the pilots to at least avoid the west side where their ledge was located. [83]

> "Hey, we're dead anyway.... might as well take some of them with us," thought Daniel. [53]

Four A-1 Skyraiders soon roared overhead, blasting the area with rockets, bombs and their 20mm cannons. Ken Woods and Rusty Irons, upon getting the urgent rescue call at Long Cheng, quickly jumped into their Air America helicopter. The Huey was normally based out of Udon Thani but happened to be nearby, Irons having flown a resupply mission to LS-85 just the day before. A distance away, they could observe smoke billowing from the top of Phou Pha Thi. When they got closer, Etchberger popped a smoke grenade to better indicate their position while the A-1s briefly held off their attacks. Irons operated the onboard winch directing so that pilot Woods could get more closer to the awaiting men. The men, still alive, were seriously injured with Daniel being shot in both legs. Etchberger miraculously remained unscathed. [83]

By then, it was about 7:30 in the morning as Richard Etchberger, while fully exposing himself to the commandos' gunfire, helped Daniel get onto the Jungle Penetrator. Essentially, it was a metal device that opened up allowing a person to straddle it while being winched up. [53]

# Part Four (1966-1976)

> "I'll be right up. I'll see you in a minute," Etchberger
> told Daniel as he went back to firing his rifle at the
> commandos. [83]

Etchberger, again exposing himself, then assisted Sliz onto the contraception for his trip aboard the Huey. No sooner was that done then William Husband ran out from nowhere towards Etchberger, so they were winched up together. Woods, by now, was quite anxious to get his chopper out of there as the small arms fire picked up in intensity.

> "To me, it seemed like the extraction took an eternity
> although it really lasted only about five minutes," Ken
> Woods later recalled. [53, 83]

As Woods lifted to fly away, a burst of gunshots blasted up from below, leaving several visible holes in the chopper's floor. Shortly into the flight, Etchberger slumped over against Irons' shoulder and Irons noticed blood on the floor where Etchberger had been sitting. The men in the helicopter couldn't quite figure out what had happened as he had no visible wounds. They found out later that one of those floor rounds had perforated his rectum and gone up into his body. Etchberger, who had just saved his injured companions at the risk of his own life, was now dead. Ultimately, only eight of the 19 men survived that day, including the two CIA agents. [53, 83]

Richard Etchberger was a 35-year-old Chief Master Sergeant, the Air Force's highest NCO rank and was awarded the Air Force Cross. It was the highest award the Air Force felt, at the time, it could bestow given the secrecy of the project. Many Vietnam and Laos war documents were kept classified until the late 1970s or early 80s. Information regarding the covert MSQ-77 operation, known as "Heavy Green", was finally released in 1988, whereupon efforts were made to more properly recognize Etchburger's bravery. In September 2010, over four decades following his death, CMsgt Richard Etchberger was posthumously awarded the Congressional Medal of Honor. The nation's top award was among only a few ever given to an enlisted airman who wasn't a pilot. [53, 79, 83]

Twenty days after the fall of Lima Site-85, President Johnson decided to limit the bombing of Hanoi. In November 1968, just eight months later, the program was terminated entirely, although bombing of the Hanoi area resumed in later years.

Phou Pha Thi, Laos (1968)

# Vermont State Hospital

When she woke up, she was lying naked on the floor. There was no bed, no mattress and not even a blanket. There wasn't even a toilet and she had to relieve herself remaining in the same tiny room with her own excrement. Her arms were kept tightly bound behind her back, both day and night. It was a painful restraint from which she just could not get any relief, no matter what position she tried to put herself in.

> "It was a physically agonizing and degrading experience. I would often hear frightening screams and shrieks coming from outside the room. Being secluded in this room went on for 14 days straight, and it happened On three separate occasions." [45]

She would be administered electric shock treatments. The chart indicated that she received eight treatments, with each one involving up to 35 shocks. The standard duration of a single shock is a fraction of a second. Her particular chart showed that shocks were being maintained for over 40 seconds at a time. [45]

> "I would be also given injections of drugs such as Trilafon, Compazine, Sodium Amytal. I was having severe allergic reactions to these drugs which created spasms in the muscles of my face and extremities. I was also administered Mellarill from which I sustained a toxic reaction." [45]

The young girl, at the time, was only 13 years old and her name was Karen. This didn't happen in some faraway Communist prison camp: it took place right here in America, during the 1960s.

The MK-ULTRA Program had its origins with Project Bluebird and later Project Artichoke. The CIA said they started the program after American POW pilots returned from the Korean War stating that they'd been involved in germ warfare. These were deemed to be false confessions as a result of being brainwashed by their Chinese captors. The CIA and military became intrigued enough to explore the possibility of using similar methods to also create human "robots" who could be trained to kill or perform other abhorrent tasks and then have no memory of what they had done. Dr. Sydney Gottleib was put in charge in July 1951 by Director Allen Dulles and by the late 1950s and 1960s, the program, under one name or another, was in full swing. [29, 81]

MK-ULTRA, itself had 149 subprograms with four of these involving children. Lysegic Acid Diethylamide (LSD) was commonly used but it wasn't the only drug or method tested. In fact, about 129 drugs were experimented with by the US Army, Public Health Service and over 80 research institutions paid by the CIA using the cover "Human Ecology Fund." One research organization was Ravenscrag at McGill University in Montreal. Nine previous patients at Ravenscrag ended up suing for unauthorized experimentation that was done on them. The CIA settled their cases out of court. [29, 81]

Karen Wetmore was held in sub-standard conditions in the hospital ward while the experiments continued until October 1970. All the while she was being denied visitation from her worried mother. In December 1970, Karen was transferred back down into the bowels of the hospital, to that tiny solitary room and kept there until June 1971. Karen was the same age as the authors of this book and could have been experiencing the same joys of graduating from high school as we did in May 1971. Instead, she was stuck in a living hell. [45]

By June 1972, CIA Director Richard Helms ordered the MK-ULTRA Program stopped and the destruction of all program documents. Karen was released from Vermont State Hospital in Waterbury that same month and it took her years to recover from her mental illness by which time she also filed a lawsuit. It was settled short of trial for a sizable sum, once it became also known that one of her own doctors had also been sexually abusing her. [45]

Other notorious research cases involved bacterial attacks by the US Army on the American public. One of 293 attacks between 1950 and 1969, was the spraying of San Francisco in 1950 without the consent or knowledge of the public, producing clouds of two different pathogens extending two miles in length. Nearly everyone in San Francisco received a dose of 500 particle minutes per liter.... every single day for a week of testing. Eleven people became seriously ill and another died. Not to be outdone by the Army, the CIA in 1955 similarly sprayed whooping cough bacteria over Tampa Bay. Subsequent incidents of whooping cough in the area increased threefold and deaths tenfold. [29, 81]

Dr. Colin Ross, M.D. in his book, *The CIA Doctors: Human Rights Violations by American Psychiatrists* makes a valid point. He states:

> "In the interests of national security, it's important that the CIA and military intelligence agencies have programs in place. There is also nothing wrong with the intelligence agencies seeking the assistance of physicians in such programs. The problem is, however, the conflict between the National Security Act and the Hippocratic Oath."

He states that how this conflict should be resolved or regulated he's not sure and doesn't offer a solution. However, he adds that "to date, organized medicine has behaved as if this conflict doesn't even exist." [28]

# Precious Treasure Island

"The long solitary hours I spent in prison gave me a new and deeper belief. My faith changed from a talisman against fear to the stoic serenity that ultimately my fate was in God's hands, not my captors'. But faith gave me the strength to endure prison." [6]

- John T. Downey (prison -year 17)

Precious Treasure Island almost sparked the start of World War III. This tiny one-third square mile, uninhabited island in the middle of the Ussari River is known as Damansky Island in Russia and called Zhenbao or Precious Treasure Island in China. International convention says the boundary between the USSR and China runs through the middle of the wide Ussari River located near Mongolia so, barring an agreement otherwise, the island should also be split as well. The two countries, however, saw the island exclusively as their own. Soviet border guards began patrolling the area back in 1947. Mao used it in 1969 as a pretext to pick a fight.

The relationship between China and the Soviet Union had been gradually worsening ever since Stalin's death in 1953. Mao felt Joseph Stalin was following the true Marxist-Leninist path, whereas Khrushchev deviated from it by denouncing Stalin and his abuse of powers at the Twentieth Soviet Congress in February 1956. He waited three years due to the powerful hold that Stalin still had on many, even after his death.

# Part Four (1966-1976)

> "During his reign, mass arrests and deportation of thousands and thousands of people, and executions without trial or normal investigation, created insecurity, fear and even desperation," Khrushchev bellowed for four hours, with only one intermission. [25]

He even attacked Stalin's war record, saying Stalin never visited the front line. Many in the secret plenum listened silently, some shocked but many others knew deep down he was right. They were just too afraid to express similar sentiments. Mao, however, viewed Khrushchev's departure from traditional communist dogma as sacrilege, in part because Mao himself relied on methods similar to Stalin's to stay in power. For example, periodic purges, personal cult building, absence of rule of law. In fact, a perfect example being the Cultural Revolution which was taking place at same the time. [25]

By 1969, Nikita Khrushchev had been out of power for about five years. Ousted in a palace coup back in October 1964 when Presidium members, many of them friends such as Leonid Brezhnev and proteges he had mentored over the years, denounced and removed Khrushchev from office. Accusations included such things as not consulting with others, berating comrades, often being erratic or explosive and bungling the 1956 Suez Crisis, the Berlin Crisis, and even "juggling the fate of the world" with the Cuban Missile Crisis. The denunciations hurt Khrushchev deeply and profoundly but he chose not to fight to remain in office. [25, 81]

The Cuban crisis in late 1962 would become the last straw, by making the Soviet Union look bad in the eyes of the world... putting in missiles able to reach American cities in Cuba and then withdrawing them when Kennedy confronted him. What the world didn't know was at the time the US had previously staged fifteen Jupiter medium-range missiles in Izmir Turkey capable of reaching Moscow. The deal with Kennedy was that the US would pull out the Jupiters if the Khruschev first removed his Cuban missiles. However, the Turkish removal was to remain confidential, so the world and an angry Castro simply saw an irresolute Khruschev in retreat. The US suffered no loss by the withdrawal as it already had in play launch platforms of Polaris missiles on submarines. After

Cuba, the die was largely cast to remove Khruschev. His long-time friend, Brezhnev, took over the reins with Aleksei Kosygin appointed as Premier. From Mao's perspective, things hadn't really changed that much to mend the Sino-Soviet split. In fact, Mao kept up the frosty relations and hadn't spoken to Brezhnev even once during the prior three years. [25, 81]

An implicit goal of the Cultural Revolution had been to rid China of Soviet-style "revisionists", hence people Mao deemed a threat to his own power more than to the system itself. What better example, he thought, than having a small military victory over a small non-descript piece of land and showing the Russkies who really had the better communist system. Participants at the upcoming Ninth Congress in Beijing set for April 1969 were sure to be impressed. On March 2, the Chinese, using a trained elite unit, laid an ambush at the island leaving thirty-two Russian soldiers dead. In retaliation, on March 14th, the Russians brought in heavy artillery and tanks and pounded the Chinese who were then compelled to cease their aggression. Ultimately, 92 Russians and several hundred Chinese soldiers were killed during the two-week period. Mao hadn't expected such a ferocious response and soon harbored fears the Russians would be invading China. [1, 81]

Months later, the Russians attacked again, this time far to the west, on the Kazakhstan–Xinjiang border, where they had huge logistical advantages. Numerous Russian tanks and armored vehicles drove deep inside China, surrounding and destroying the Chinese troops. Lop Nur, in Xinjiang was where China conducted its nuclear testing including their first atomic bomb in 1964 followed by the hydrogen bomb just two years later. To the Russians, taking back Precious Treasure Island was less important than national pride and honor. The Russian bear had been poked and Mao now became seriously worried about a strike against his atomic installations. Installations he coveted, waited years to obtain and which the Soviet Union actually helped him develop back in 1959. [1]

About this time, the death of another communist leader brought about a sense of reason to the belligerents. Ho Chi Minh passed away later that September

## Part Four (1966-1976)

and many attended his funeral in Hanoi, including Kosygin and Zhou Enlai, making sure, of course, not to be there at the same time. Any messages between them were transmitted via the North Vietnamese who they both continued to support despite the ongoing rift. Kosygin would fly back to Moscow but was forced to take a longer route as China wouldn't allow his flight through its airspace. When Kosygin had to land to take on more fuel in Calcutta, he received a message saying China wanted a discussion to talk peace. Meeting Kosygin at the Beijing airport lounge, Zhou sought assurances from Moscow that it wouldn't launch a nuclear attack. Kosygin, however, gave him no such guarantee at the time. In a couple months time, the countries exchanged ambassadors and conducted border discussions. While nevertheless confident there would be no war, Mao kept up the war rhetoric at home as it supported his Superpower Program for modernizing Chinese weaponry. [1, 81]

As part of the Tibet Program, early U2 flights were conducted over Xinjiang Province. Naturally, this monitoring of what was happening at Lop Nur Test Base helped the CIA predict the first atomic bombs tests in October 1964. Lop Nur was 750 miles north of Lhasa and seemed unrelated to the agency's assistance to achieve Tibetan independence. That said, in 1969, the CIA trained Tibetan Amdo Tsering in intelligence gathering since his mission was to obtain radioactive soil samples from the Lop Nur area. While enroute to the distant nuclear base, he unfortunately attracted suspicion and was captured by the Chinese. The CIA relied solely on U2 overflights thereafter. [81]

Today, Precious Treasure Island belongs to China... finally concluding over three decades of border negotiations with their on and off again communist friends to the north.

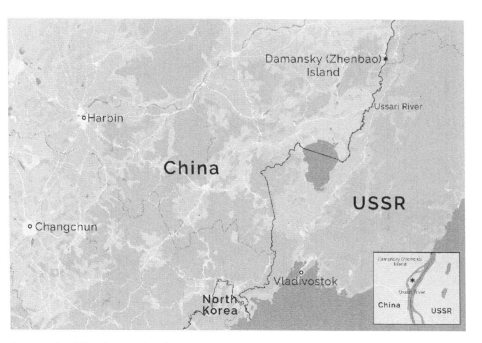

Damansky (Zhenbao) Island (1969)

# Reversal of Fortune

With respect to the Tibetan Program, Richard Helms took over as Director of the CIA in 1966 and was quite skeptical of covert action programs similar to it. Subordinates had bent his ear to hang with it; however, when Desmond Fitzgerald passed away, the program lost its primary booster, leading to further disengagement. The US decided to terminate funding of eight Tibetan students attending Cornell University and the $180,000 yearly stipend paid to the Dalai Lama's charitable trust was also stopped. On top of that, Baba Yeshi, who commanded the Tibetan guerrillas in Mustang and had been producing lackluster results in recent years, was also believed to be skimming funds. In 1969, the CIA had already decided to cut the number of guerrillas in Mustang that it was subsidizing. The handwriting was already on the wall as to discontinuation of funding the Tibetan Program by the time of Nixon's rapprochement with Mao.

The Secret War in Laos was another ballgame altogether. Tony Poe took charge of a large northwest area having minimal combat with the enemy except sporadic Pathet Lao skirmishing. He commanded a hodge-podge of six thousand armed ethnic fighters. Fighters who, in the absence of a true enemy, chose instead to fight amongst each other. He had Lao Theung, Lahu, Hmong, Shan, Wa Tai Dam, lowland Lao and Thai PARU. The most numerous minority was the Yao, also known as the Mien. To calm the infighting, Poe had separate mess halls built for each group at his base in Nam Yu. American paid for weapons, seldom used, that began showing up on the black market. Mao's forces weren't that far away as they were building the Chinese Road from Yunnan to the Mekong River. A possible invasion route? Maybe not, but they always fired at US reconnaissance flights that were overhead, monitoring their progress. The CIA also tapped certain phone lines inside China, although the information obtained was of marginal benefit. [23, 24]

Tony Poe settled his wife and the children in Udorn and made a point of visiting once a month. Life was tedious and boring aside from the internal conflicts, so much so that Poe stepped up his drinking. He lived in a thatched hut without any of the amenities of Long Cheng, such as hot showers. His most loyal men stood continuous armed guard around his hut, often sleeping on mats laid on the ground. He put out a bounty on Pathet Lao; after all, they had a bounty on him. He told his fighters he would pay 5,000 kip for a pair of Communist ears. Author Steven Schofield recalls visiting Poe at Nam Yu... [24]

> "Upon arrival, Tony took me into the room that held his cot and pointed out the very large jar full of pickled ears that sat on a table next to the cot. Tony confirmed enemy killed and also paid his troops 'bonuses based on body counts. Later, the story goes, he stopped this practice when he found a local twelve-year-old boy with his ears cut off." [24]

Apparently, the boy's father, desperate for money, saw a way to cash in. Poe denied, however, collecting heads and pickling them in jars. although he did admit to twice hurling human heads from an aircraft down onto his enemies in Laos, just to terrify them. He disavowed many other bar stories or legends attributed to him and cutting off ears was not something contrived by Tony Poe in Laos. As he related to author Richard Ehrlich:

> "We cut the ears off of enemy Japanese in World War II with a K-bar knife on Iwo Jima." [109]

Removing enemy body parts was actually not an uncommon practice by US ground forces in the Pacific theater. It included skulls, bones but frequently gold teeth and, in particular, ears which were easily removed. In the Philippines,

# Part Four (1966-1976)

during the war, Muslim guerrillas were known to slice off Japanese ears and exchange them for bullets or cash from US guerrilla leader Colonel Fertig. Wendell Fertig had faced issues and controversies, similar to that experienced later by Tony Poe, when uniting and incentivizing guerrilla forces on Mindanao. The concept wasn't a new one but it did have later consequences. [81]

Of course, Tony Poe was now operating near the beating heart of the opium network, the Golden Triangle. By the mid-1960s, the trade changed dramatically when US troops created an expansive new market. Most of the opium was produced in Burma and Laos with shipments transiting through Laos. The Royalist commander in chief, General Ouane Rattikone, was at the center of a power pyramid involved with various illicit activities besides opium. Whatever portion Ouane got, the King also received his slice. Ouane largely left the Hmong alone to handling their opium trade in northeast Laos as he needed to keep Vang Pao happy so he expanded his own base by purchasing more from the Burmese. After all, the sizable market now could accommodate several major players. Tony Poe was asked by the agency to keep an eye on Ouane's opium business but that would prove to be most difficult given its size and changing character. Moreover, there was a war still going which Poe had to contend with. [38]

Vang Pao allowed raw opium to be sold in the Long Cheng market. Others said he was more of an active participant in the drug business, as Tony Poe himself asserted. Poe's perspective may be tainted by the somewhat harsh opinions he already harbored for Vang. That said, it was known that Vang had about a ton of opium stashed underneath his house in Long Cheng. Other viewpoints maintained that Vang Pao didn't need the proceeds derived from opium sales as he was already benefitting by skimming from salaries the CIA was paying his Hmong soldiers. After all, it was relatively easy to claim soldiers killed in combat as being still listed on the active roll. In reality, the truth involved some measure of all the opinions. [23, 24]

As shown with Vang Pao, Baba Yeshe and others before them, disbursements were often made by the CIA with little regard to standards ensuring proper accountability, let alone prevention of fraud. In Nam Yu, planes came in once a month with bags of cash but it was never enough for Poe to get his fighters to work together. The annual payments made to the Dalai Lama charitable trust was known to be used for investments, donations and unrelated matters. The money spigot was cranked open and usually left in that position.

> "If you knew how much we spend, and how much money we waste in this area, it would knock you off your chair. It's criminal!"
>
> - Senator Allen Ellender, Chairman of Intelligence Subcommittee-1971 [88]

Congress, as a whole, made no appropriation to the CIA. The agency's funds were covertly transferred from the appropriations made to other government entities. The Government Accountability Office (GAO), often known as the "congressional watchdog", had broad authority to evaluate CIA programs. In reality there are limitations, for instance it had no access to "unvouchered accounts" and GAO audits of the CIA ceased in the early 1960s when the CIA prevented access to information necessary to conduct an audit. The Central Intelligence Agency Act of 1949 authorized the CIA to secretly fund intelligence operations and conduct personnel actions outside of standard U.S. Government procedures. From the agency's perspective, seeking alternative sources for secret programs to make up for any deficits in funding also seemed warranted. [2]

Meanwhile, back in Laos with its flourishing opium trade, ethnic infighting, excessive drinking and corpse mutilation... the war went on. Pressure was being brought to bear on Long Cheng by the North Vietnamese. The world's most secret place in a secret war was really not so much of a secret after all. It certainly wasn't a secret to the enemy as they've known it was there back to after they took Ban Pa Dong from Vang Pao years before. It wasn't a secret from Congress. Congressmen Pete McCloskey, Olin Teague and others were given private tours in Laos. Senator Stuart Symington certainly knew as he tried to get Laos spending under control. It was just the American public that didn't know, at least not yet.

The last two years of the 1960s were considered the worst in Vietnam and also in the secret war in Laos. Eighteen thousand Hmong soldiers were killed and scores more civilians just in that period alone. Replacement troops were harder to obtain. As Pop Buell, of USAID, said in 1968:

> "A short time ago, we rounded up 300 fresh recruits. Thirty percent were 14 years old or less and 10 of them were 10 years old. Another 30 percent were 15 or 16 years old. The remaining 40 percent were 45 or older. Where were the ones in between? I'll tell you.... they are all dead!" [34]

The war was taking a heavy toll on the Hmong families. By 1970, the average age among Hmong recruits was approaching fifteen years old. As Colonel Walter Boyne in 1970 said:

> "Air America was keeping 170,000 Hmong refugees alive with airdrops of rice. A situation that's been going on so long that children were said to believe rice was not grown but it simply fell from the sky." [34]

One of the stated missions of the Laos war had evolved into stopping the North Vietnamese from sending troops and supplies down the Ho Chi Minh trail. It was really no longer a war about working in concert with Laos Royalists to free the country from the communists. To get his needed recruits, Vang Pao's recruiters occasionally threatened to have rice drops stopped if his Hmong didn't come up with more recruits — a policy apparently also supported by US officials. Families had to give up their young sons to ensure the rest of the brood could be fed. However, as the war went on, more families simply refused.

Then in March 1970, the North Vietnamese attacked Long Cheng where thousands of Hmong had chosen to make their home. Vang Pao pleaded for reinforcements to defend "Shangri-La", with Tony Poe and others answering the call. He sent companies of mostly Yao, who couldn't speak the Hmong language. It wasn't long before shots were about to be fired by the Yao and Poe had to point a .30-caliber Browning heavy machine gun at them. Using an interpreter, he yelled: [33, 34]

"PUT THOSE FUCKIN GUNS ON THE GROUND, RIGHT NOW!!"

They sheepishly laid down their weapons and headed back to the plane for a quick return trip to Nam Yu. Instead of saving the day, Poe's forces from the northwest turned out to be a major embarrassment which reflected badly on him. The overarching concept that they were all fighting for the same country was lost on the Yao. It wasn't long before Tony Poe was removed from Laos and transferred to take over training of Tom Fosmire's old camp at Phitsanulok in Thailand. By 1970, Fosmire was in Vietnam working under Ted Shackley who had taken over as Chief of Saigon Station. [34]

# Beyond the Skyline

After giving a rousing speech, the Mexican guerrilla chief charged uphill with his twelve hundred fighters, enduring withering fire. "Whisssshing," the bullets began zinging past them left and right, some high a few low..... but many would find their mark and men quickly dropped. Over a hundred of them would become casualties in just the first five minutes alone. This Tony Poe incarnation was Elias Chavez, CIA knuckle dragger dressed in poncho, cross-chest bandoliers with a Catholic cross clenched between his teeth. His Hmong and Thai warriors, while not fully grasping the Mexican connection, were greatly inspired, nonetheless. [23]

Over the next three days, the now partly decimated band moved relentlessly towards the North Vietnamese positions as Chavez, tossing hand grenades, urged them on. Near the top of the ridge, the fighting became much more intense resulting in vicious hand to hand combat. American planes overhead reported seeing blood and body parts splattered extensively across the rocks below. The fight went on nonstop for over a week. The much-vaunted North Vietnamese Army finally ended up retreating due to the ferocity of Chavez's Banditos. [23]

At one point near the end, a sizable group of escaping Vietnamese soldiers were noticed getting stuck in a thicket of bamboo which they tried to hack through. Machine guns and also Vang Pao's artillery from below trained their sights on that area, and let loose. When the battle finally concluded, three thousand enemy soldiers lay dead, yet Hanoi still desperately wanted Skyline Ridge, the gateway to Long Cheng.

After a lull of several weeks, the North Vietnamese would bring forth their latest war gadgetry, Soviet built tanks, which scared the hell out of Hmong fighters who didn't know how to fight them. The tanks, however, ultimately fell victim to land mines and bombing by American planes, not to mention extreme difficulty they had in traversing steep muddy slopes. On some roads and pathways, disabled tanks blocked the others from getting through. The T-34s were great for level-ground warfare but grossly unsuitable for the rugged terrain that surrounded Long Cheng. [33]

This was the third and biggest battle for Skyline Ridge. If it held and Long Cheng was protected, then the road to Laos' capital, Vientiane, was secure. More succinctly, if Skyline fell, it would be game over for non-communist Laos. Realizing the threat to its own country, Thailand contributed troops under the Unity program, financed by the CIA, which augmented the Vang Pao's fighters at Long Cheng. Several Thai battalions, including artillery, were sent to Long Cheng later supplemented by more including those sent to Military Region 4 in the south. The Thais made up for much of the depletion that had occurred in the Hmong ranks. In their initial attempt during the first three months of 1970, the North Vietnamese made it as far as the ridgeline but ended up backing down prior to onset of the coming monsoon season. In the early months of the following year, they tried once again. Thai troops and American bombing forced them to again retreat after getting in close enough range to lob artillery shells into Long Cheng, damaging Vang Pao's house and other structures. By late 1971, the enemy's Campaign Z commenced, their third attempt to take Long Cheng. Four thousand Hmong, lowland Lao, Thai and CIA advisors faced down twenty battalions of North Vietnamese. The defenders were now out numbered by a ratio of six to one. [33, 81]

Campaign Z ended up failing as well despite the T-34 tanks, long range heavy artillery and increased number of combat soldiers. North Vietnam was about to kick off their massive Easter Offensive in South Vietnam and chose to divert two divisions to that effort. Of the twenty-three thousand troops the communists dedicated to assaulting Skyline Ridge, ten thousand ended up being killed or wounded. Most of the casualties resulted from on-call bombing by US Air Force planes, including B-52 bombers. One sortie of three big-belly B-52Ds alone caught the 866th NVA Regiment out in the open and decimated it. Raven forward air controllers flying their Cessnas and Henry Kissinger now authorizing the CIA to directly request B-52 missions went a long way to improving bombing effectiveness. The Battle for Skyline Ridge went down as being the biggest battle of the  entire Vietnam War. [33]

> "Realizing that we no longer had a chance of liberating Long Cheng, the Campaign Command Headquarters decided to bring the campaign to an end on April 5, 1972. This may have been the only time during the entire history of our Vietnamese Volunteer Army's combat operations in Laos that we suffered such heavy casualties and were still not able to achieve victory." [33]
>
> - Lieutenant General Tran Thu, North Vietnamese Army

Bravery and a staunch defense does not win a war, however. The Paris Peace Talks, which began in 1968, was by May 1972 finally beginning to bear fruit. Hanoi would soon balk, however, leaving Nixon to pressure them with the Operation Linebacker bombing campaign over North Vietnam. A ceasefire was finally called by early January 1973, followed a week later with the official signing of the peace accords.

Laos was left out of the process and advised to make their own pact with the Pathet Lao. This didn't sit well with Laos, considering the country had been intimately tied to the Vietnam War and the belligerents in both conflicts were largely the same. Prime Minister Souvanna Phouma refused to publicly acknowledge the Paris Accords, let alone wanted to cut a separate deal. Henry Kissinger, however, strongly advised the Lao government to negotiate a ceasefire and told them that US financial support would be winding down. Just as in Tibet earlier, the US was now making its exit stage left while closing off the money pipeline in the process. Souvanna relented and the Vientiane Treaty, signed a month after the Paris Accords, required that a coalition government which included the Pathet Lao be set up. [23]

Vang Pao, with his remaining ten thousand men, did not give up the fight but it was a losing effort since, without strong air support, he lost battle after battle. By the end of 1974, the North Vietnamese sat comfortably on top of Skyline Ridge, simply waiting. Within a year's time, Laos like Vietnam, would completely succumb to communism.

The CIA often points to the secret war in Laos with pride. Richard Helms governed the agency during its heyday, whereas William Colby took over in 1975. Both men considered the war a resounding success. Helms stated: [23]

> "The agency had proven itself in warfare and held off communism far more effectively than even the US military." [23]

> "The secret war had occupied seventy thousand North Vietnamese troops who might otherwise have fought Americans in Vietnam," Colby later added. [23]

The paramilitary programs were considered the most successful the agency had ever mounted and, throughout the conflict, they perfected their war fighting skills that proved most useful in future endeavors. These were all true and valid points when measured against isolated and albeit self-serving benchmarks. This also is not to take anything away from the valiant, hard working CIA agents and agency contractors. However, when compared to the primary goal of ensuring Laos neutrality by keeping out communism, the agency failed. To say it also saved American lives by keeping North Vietnamese divisions busy is arguably disingenuous. It implied that Hmong deaths were a beneficial sacrifice or byproduct belying their own objectives and reason for fighting.

To use an indigenous people for a wartime purpose, where almost 10% of the population died while leading the way to its possible extinction by depleting its male population, is patently wrong. On a per capita basis, more Hmong were killed in the war than either Americans or Japanese died in World War II. In fact, many more Hmong civilians perished than did their actual combatants, albeit from increased American bombing. [23, 81]

On the basis of promises or representations made, and Hmong's reliance on those promises, there was also a failure. Maybe more so than with the Tibetan Program. In the latter, Tibetans came to believe the CIA would help them achieve their independence from China. The agency denied they made any such representations but they also weren't clear with the Tibetans about their true agenda. After all, they needed the Tibetans to be their proxies for harassing and spying on the Chinese. Had they told the Tibetans that's what they were only needed for, the latter likely wouldn't have gone along with the program. In Laos, a more succinct promise was actually made to the Hmong:

> "We may not win this war and if not, we will take care of you." [110]

The CIA and the White House only approved giving asylum to Vang Pao and his immediate family. The clandestine officers still left in Laos several times requested airlifts for the Lao and Hmong similar to that provided to escaping Vietnamese. The answer each time was a resounding, "No." It seemed Congress had passed a law helping the Vietnamese but not the Hmong. This answer was not acceptable to a number of CIA operatives, Air American pilots and contractors. Without getting official permission, they did their own airlift, ferrying out 2,500 Hmong to safety in Thailand. Twenty-five thousand Hmong, not fortunate enough to get on one of those freedom flights, set out on foot on a perilous journey towards Thailand. [81]

In May 1975, two weeks after Vang Pao's plane flew him out to safety, up to three thousand Hmong civilians began the long trek towards Ban Sorn which led to Vientiane and Thailand. With children crying, they carried their blankets, pans and sundries on their backs through jungle, over hills and across rivers. Many fell victim to disease, hunger and ambush along the way. They finally gathered en masse to cross the bridge at Hin Heup, not far from Vientiane. Near the end of their arduous journey and within grasp of freedom, the unspeakable was about to happen. [23, 81]

> "With little warning, Pathet Lao troops near the bridge opened fire on the Hmong families, killing many. Some of the soldiers attacked the families with machine guns, heavier guns, and knives"

> "Mortars hit us and some soldiers charged, bayoneting people. I tried to run and jumped over seven or eight bodies lying on the road as I tried to get over the bridge," recalled Vang Teng, former officer in Vang Pao's army. [23]

After the dust had settled, fourteen Hmong civilians lay dead and over one hundred were injured. Hin Heup was not an isolated incident: within two years after the signing of the Vientiane Treaty and even after the communist takeover in 1975, the Pathet Lao singled out the Hmong so severely that some experts on Laos have called it a post-war genocide. Aside from repeated torture and summary executions, the Pathet Lao were known to toss Hmong into a hole in the ground, leaving them there to die of starvation. Tony Poe certainly did the Hmong no favors with his policy of cutting off ears and tossing heads from airplanes. The enemy knew, after all, a bounty had been put on Poe's own head years previously. Vang Pao's ill treatment of communist prisoners was also not a hidden secret. War memories can linger a very long time.... [23]

Most others who escaped Pathet Lao's brutality ended up in the Ban Vinai camp in Thailand near its border with Laos. The over-crowded refugee camp, housing over 40,000 Hmong at its peak, had no electricity, running water or sewage disposal but it was, however, safe from Pathet Lao bent on retribution. By 1975, the US began accepting a small number of Hmong refugees and in 1980, it passed legislation allowing a greater yearly influx of Hmong immigrants into the country. Ninety percent of the Hmong chose to go live in the United States, the country they fought with and died for. [23, 81]

Long Cheng Region, Laos (early 1970s)

# Spies Among Us

The year 1967 was a notable for several events in the espionage world. John Anthony Walker, a Navy warrant officer, began helping the Soviets decrypt more than a million naval messages and headed a spy ring which included his seaman son, Michael Walker. The Secretary of the Navy later said that Walker allowed the Soviet Union to know where every US submarine was located negating the stealth advantage of subs carrying Poseidon nuclear missiles. It was also the year that Operation CHAOS was started by the CIA to spy domestically on political movements thought to have been instigated or supported by foreign entities. President Johnson had requested the agency initiate a program similar yet separate from COINTELPRO which the FBI had been running since 1956. The man selected to get CHAOS going was James Jesus Angelton, head of counter-intelligence at the agency. Its original mission was to target anti-Vietnam war groups but the scope later expanded to include Jewish organizations, Black Panther Party and the Women's Liberation movement. When Nixon came into office, he expanded the program further notwithstanding likely violations of the CIA's original charter which barred domestic operations. [81]

The person in charge became the master of paranoia himself who, for a number of years, believed the agency was being infiltrated by KGB spies. James Angelton's clandestine leanings began back with the OSS in Italy where he first made a name for himself during the second World War. After the war, he participated in several organizations that later became the CIA in 1947 and was considered one of its founders. During the 1940s, the Venona Project came into being as a counterintelligence attempt to decrypt messages routinely transmitted by Soviet intelligence agencies. Started by the Army's Signal Intelligence Service, it later came under the purview of the National Security Agency. Paranoia was not without justification during the forties and early fifties as Venona revealed Soviet espionage was deeply involved with the Manhattan Project leading to their own atomic test in 1949. Unsurprisingly, their device was substantially similar in design to the Fat Man bomb which was dropped on Nagasaki. [81]

As the CIA was coming into being, the Chinese had its own spy agency called the Central Social Affairs Department (SAD) which became the Central Investigations Department (CID) in 1955. Headed by Kang Sheng, who became Mao's henchman not unlike what sadistic Lavrentiy Beria was to Stalin. During the Cultural Revolution, Kang was the silent hand behind the Case Examination Group involved in many of the purges of high party officials. Kang Sheng's coup de grace was his early support for the Khymer Rouge, whose later fanaticism lead to mass genocide in Cambodia. Kang was initially trained by the Soviets but would augment that training with his own style of brutality. [81]

It wasn't the Chinese CID that preoccupied the agency's concerns during the early years but rather the Soviets. The Soviet intelligence service beginning in 1954 was governed by the KGB (Committee for State Security) which had been preceded by the NKVD. Their competing service was the GRU which came under military command, is actually much larger and takes on tasks akin to the paramilitary elements of the CIA. During the first thirty years of the Cold War, the US was predominately concerned with KGB attempts to obtain the wherewithal to build nuclear weapons and infiltrate select US organizations. They also tried to obtain classified secrets of the newly established NATO, including its plans, procedures and weaknesses. The KGB's primary means of success in recruiting new contacts was by working in tandem with the American Communist Party. In fact, most all agents in the US involved referrals from the party. There were "legal" agents who were under cover and protection of diplomatic immunity should they happen to get caught. The illegal agents, however, were far more prolific in producing "actionable" information. [81]

Angelton was named by Allen Dulles to take over the CIA's counterintelligence operations in 1954 and would later find himself at the center of two high profile Soviet defections. Western intelligence agencies, in particular, the CIA, didn't always have the best of luck infiltrating the Soviet Union, so when high-value defectors decided to "cross over", it became a godsend; although, extra care was necessary to ensure they weren't double agents. Anatoliy Golitsyn was the first important defection during Angelton's watch in 1961. Golitsyn would become somewhat controversial, however, as some described him as an "unreliable conspiracy theorist" while others like author John Hackett and Angelton felt he was "the most valuable defector to ever reach the West." Particularly disturbing was Golitsyn's suggestion that British Prime Minister Harold Wilson was a KGB informer and an "agent of influence." Wilson did have Russian contacts from his many trade missions to the USSR but several investigations by Mi-6 cleared his name. Importantly, Golitsyn's defection set into motion an inquiry process that determined it was really Kim Philby who was a Soviet mole. [81]

Harold "Kim" Philby was a British intelligence agent being groomed to take over the Special Investigation Service (also known as MI-6) one day. He was assigned in 1949 as first Secretary for the British Embassy in Washington and as the primary liaison with American intelligence services. It's where he got to know Angelton and actually was credited with teaching Angelton the tradecraft of counterintelligence. Both were educated in England and had very similar literary tastes, including a love of poetry and penchant for French wine, and German music. Running in the same social circles, they ended up becoming colleagues and very close friends.

Then in 1951, Philby was implicated as being a Soviet agent but was exonerated four years later. He was implicated yet again in 1963 after having relayed thousands of documents to the communists over many years. Philby then fled to Moscow to live out his remaining life, leaving Angelton crushed, both personally and professionally. From that point on, he could hardly trust anyone, particularly when Yur Nosenko defected to the US in 1963. Nosenko spent three years in various forms of detention, including solitary because Angelton distrusted whether he was a bonafide defector. Nosenko was finally released by the CIA Director who provided him also with a new identity and compensation for the harsh treatment that he endured. [81]

A chastened and paranoid counterintelligence chief was the perfect person to seek his redemption by taking on Operation CHAOS. A project which infiltrated domestic antiwar organizations and worked with college administrators and local police to identify antiwar dissidents. Under the HT LINGUAL portion of CHAOS, the CIA opened and examined correspondence between the US and USSR as well as China from 1952 until 1973. Over the course, 215,000 letters were opened and scrutinized at CIA facilities located on both coasts. Mail that was examined included correspondence from Bobby Fischer, Martin Luther King, John Steinbeck and Hubert Humphrey. No foreign influence was ever to be found. [81, 92]

James Angelton also directed his "mole hunt" inward on the CIA itself. For several years, the agency's personnel were put under intense scrutiny with a number of agents' careers ending up falsely derailed. He even checked into the lives of their spouses and children. Angelton became increasingly convinced that the CIA was compromised by the KGB. He believed the later Chinese/US rapprochement was orchestrated by a KGB manufactured Sino-Soviet split. Angelton even speculated whether Henry Kissinger was under the influence of the KGB. Operation CHAOS ended up being terminated in 1974 with his department reduced to a tenth of its previous size. Angelton was then forced to retire from the CIA and some of the agents who were excessively hounded were compensated for their foreshortened careers. [81, 92]

In July 1973, William Colby was appointed as the new Director of the CIA, taking over from James Schlesinger. Colby was a strong critic of Angelton's activities:

> "... maintaining that it was not the CIA's function to fight the KGB; the KGB was merely an obstacle en route to scaling the walls surrounding the Politburo and the Central Committee. But in Angelton he saw only a KGB fighter and a failed spycatcher." [92]

As Director Colby himself later pointed out:

> "I couldn't find that we ever caught a spy under Jim
> Angelton. That really bothered me." [92]

David Wise, author of *The American Police State*, said, "What was absolutely chilling was the realization that such a man could have held a high position for so long in so powerful an agency of government."

# Ping Heard Around the World

Our little Colorado school, enveloped in an alpine forest of pine and aspen, sat right at the base of Highway 24. Leaving nearby Minturn, the roadway quickly ascends in elevation, passing the historic mining towns of Gilman and Red Cliff before skirting by now defunct Camp Hale. It was the same route Ella Burnett took to visit her patients in Leadville back in 1956. During the wintertime, driving the pass can be a treacherous endeavor belying the views and stunning mountain scenery seen along the way. This was where the area's first settlers made their living carving out wealth from the mountain or running the railroad. Residents today are generations removed, yet most still know each other and their kin in some way or another. Bonds still remain strong amongst area families who lived here throughout the Cold War, often sending their young to fight and die in the deadly conflicts it spawned. This corner of Colorado is like most other small towns in America... other than, of course, it being located at an elevation almost two miles high.

It was the beginning of April 1971 and with a snowpack stubbornly refusing to melt, Battle Mountain High School was gearing up for graduation day set only a couple months away. Most of us were ordering caps and gowns, signing yearbooks and comparing colleges. I was more preoccupied with making a final mark on my high school years in the two months still remaining. After suffering a recurring foot injury the previous three years, this was now one last chance to put my stamp on school athletics, knowing I was fast provided that I remained injury free. Indeed, it would be an auspicious start, as I began winning the sprint events at track meets by early April. This would be the same small Colorado high school of thirty-four seniors that co-author Deb, Mercy Trujillo, and a year later, Charley Troxel, would all be graduating from. [79]

However, our own private worlds paled in comparison to the good fortune about to take place on the other side of the globe. Sometime during that same first week of April, another lone American athlete, a tad older than myself, got onto a bus filled with Chinese communists. No one dared talk to him and looked on with suspicion when he turned his back showing "USA" emblazoned on his warmups. Rising scorn now mixed with suspicion. *"Who is this guy?"* and *"Why the hell is he on our team bus??"* were likely the collective thoughts of the Chinese table tennis team in Nagoya, Japan. [81, 89]

The older Zhuang Zedong, three-time world champion, seated at the back of the bus took stock of the situation. He was conjuring up a multitude of reasons why he shouldn't say anything to this American. For the first almost ten minutes of the fifteen-minute ride to the stadium, no one dared speak to the long-haired foreigner. He'd be off the bus soon enough....

> "Our team had been advised not to speak to Americans, not to shake their hands, and not to exchange gifts with them," said Zhuang. "I grew up with the slogan 'Down with the American Imperialism.' [89]

> "I looked at him, thinking, *'He is not the one who makes national policies, he is simply an athlete, an ordinary American,'*" he recalled. Zhuang didn't want to get into trouble, but he thought snubbing the American went against China's tradition of hospitality. Unlike the others, he also had the moral stature and courage to do something. Something which braved against prevailing political correctness. [89]

Zhuang, dragging along the team translator, approached Glenn Cowan and started up a friendly conversation. Unsurprisingly, his teammates were somewhat aghast. Zhuang even gave the hippie-attired American a silk screen portrait of the Huangshan Mountains as a gift. Cowan, frantically searching through his bag, was unable to reciprocate. However, the next day, he handed Zhuang a T-shirt showing a peace sign and the words "LET IT BE." A message resonating as deeply as the gift exchange itself. [81, 89]

It seems Glenn Cowan had been practicing late when the training center closed. He missed his team bus and hopped aboard the next available ride, the Chinese bus. When the bus came to a stop photographers were quick to capture the moment of World Champion Zhuang Zedong conversing with the smiling American. News flashed around the world, even more so when Premier Zhou Enlai extended an invitation for the American team to visit China. The US promptly accepted it on April 7th, the very next day. Over twenty years of animosity, mistrust and isolation were suddenly shattered by the simple mistake of getting on a wrong bus and another person having the mettle to get up and talk to him. [89]

Developments increased in momentum after the US team's visit to China on April 10th.

Henry Kissinger, at Nixon's urging, had been unsuccessfully trying to open back channels to China since the fall of 1970. He would have better luck with the Pakistanis who maintained cordial relations with China. Apparently, China was leaning in a similar direction prompting the idea of a secret parley to lay the ground for a later summit between Mao and Nixon. The air needed to be cleared beforehand on sticky matters relating to Tibet, Vietnam and Taiwan. This all led the way for Kissinger's secret trip to Beijing in July. All the while, even the CIA was deliberately kept in the dark about Kissinger's secret rapprochement efforts. [20, 81]

First, however, Nixon had to deal with another explosive issue now crossing his desk — the first issue of the Pentagon Papers was posted in the New York Times on June 13th. Daniel Ellsberg, of the RAND Corporation, had been commissioned by the Defense Department to conduct a top-secret study of US decision making involving Vietnam dating back to World War II. Upon completion of the work, he was struck with an attack of moral conscience, realizing the American public needed to know what had been going on. Not unlike Zhuang Zedong, Ellsberg believed that doing the right thing outweighed the associated risks. The government tried to suppress additional release of the report, arguing that interests of national security prevailed. The matter quickly went up to the US Supreme Court and on June 30th, it ruled for the New York Times in favor of protections afforded under the First Amendment. Nixon seeing his efforts at detente with China and re-election being eroded by revelations released from the papers had his "plumbers" break into Ellsberg's psychiatrist office in September, hoping to find dirt to attack Ellsberg's credibility. Thus leading down the long and winding road to Watergate. [20, 81, 84]

While all this was going on in Washington, Kissinger held his secret confab with Zhou Enlai. Taiwan was a major topic of discussion with Enlai holding to the usual "Taiwan is a part of China" position. Kissinger didn't specifically agree but he seemed to satisfy Enlai when he responded the US wasn't advocating a two China's solution. The way was now set for Nixon's historic visit to Beijing which followed in late February 1972. China was having difficulties with the Soviet Union and was hoping detente with the US would strengthen their position. Interestingly, the US was thinking similarly, that a Soviet/Chinese split would work to its own strategic advantage. [20]

Later the same year, agent Richard Fecteau was released in December after spending nineteen years in a Chinese prison. He walked across the Lao Wu border bridge between China and Hong Kong with no one there to meet him since his release was unannounced. Throughout his captivity, the U.S. had been denying he was a CIA agent. However, U.S. officials disclosed privately that they no longer disputed Chinese charges that he was a spy. [6]

John Downey, however, wasn't released until March 11, 1973, despite Nixon's historic visit to China the year before. China still demanded that US acknowledge Downey worked for the CIA but the US, to save face, was still maintaining that Downey was a Department of Defense employee. On January 31, 1973, just four days after the signing of the Paris Peace Accords ending America's involvement in Vietnam, President Nixon held a news conference announcing the signing. The conference also discussed many other unrelated matters such as interest rates on agricultural loans.[6]

Near the end of the news conference, Nixon took a question from a reporter asking about the fate of John Downey.

> "Well, Downey is a different case, as you know," said Nixon "Downey involves a CIA agent." [6]

# End of Days

By 1972, Tony Poe had been working at Phitsanulok Camp in Thailand now for a couple years. Old hats in the clandestine service reported he would secretly pop in to Vientiane for a bender and a poke. In other words, to drink and carouse. While Poe was barred from Laos by not only the CIA but also by the Laos Coalition Government, it didn't matter. Rumor had it that an interview with Dispatch News blew the cover on Nam Yu operations so the agency decided to pull Tony Poe out. Author Steven Schofield recalled that, one day, a more rotund Tony Poe showed up at a restaurant in the Dong Phalong nightlife district wearing dark glasses and his trademark Marine Corps campaign hat. He noticed Poe was also missing two middle fingers on his left hand, a result of explosion from a booby-trapped ammo can. Tony Poe, now 52 years old, went on to retire in 1975, while continuing to live with his family in Thailand. In later years, he was often seen in the Bangkok area at Lucy's Tiger Den or the Madrid Bar trading war stories with his agency buddies. [24]

Bill Lair left Laos in 1968 and was offered an assignment with the Phoenix Program in Vietnam but declined. He stayed on in Bangkok until the end of the Vietnam War when his Thai brother-in-law was a member of a delegation which visited Mao Tse-Tung during his final days. Lair was briefed on the outcome of that visit which he relayed up the command to Henry Kissinger and the President. It included vital intel such as who would be Mao's likely successor. In 1968, the program to which Lair was offered a position was already in full swing and it may have been well he didn't accept. [51]

## Part Four (1966-1976)

Corporal Jim Richards knew the Viet Cong had been harassing one of the nearby villages, one that was very pro-Saigon. They would hit up the villages for food, rice supplies and taxes and one particular Viet Cong group was threatening the village elders. Richards 'platoon was tasked to check out the matter. As they approached the village, they heard a woman screaming...

The leader of this group of eight was a particularly cruel man who called himself General Trang but he was no general. He had told the villagers that if they didn't come up with the taxes, he was going take the chief's young daughter and make an example of her. While the parents watched in horror, he chopped off their four-year-old daughter's right leg with a machete, about four inches above the knee. Then the Viet Cong group quickly melted into the jungle.

"We called for medevac while our medic put a tourniquet on her leg.I held the little girl, who was writhing and crying out in pain. Her mother was absolutely hysterical, so much so that the medic had to sedate her. Once the chopper arrived, we bundled and secured the girl to the basket that was lowered and the chopper flew away.

"This was the saddest thing I had ever witnessed. After all that, none of us had a dry eye. Tears were running down cheeks of combat hardened soldiers who didn't even know they were crying. It was impossible to even imagine anyone inflicting such a cruel atrocity on a child. We hunted down the guerrilla band and killed six of them but Trang and his bodyguard weren't among them.

"A couple weeks passed before I was handed a M14 sniper rifle with scope by our captain. I was also given a map and instructions to meet up with another soldier, named Tom, who would be my spotter. Then I was handed a photo which was taken from flyers the Viet Cong had been posting. To my astonishment, my target was none other than Trang. I was told to memorize the face and return the photograph. How could I forget that face? It had a scar on one side near the mouth, making him appear like the Joker. Evil, it was pure evil. So off we went by chopper and then through the jungle on foot, following the map.

"Finally, we entered a clearing and I recognized Trang on the other side, speaking with some fellow cadres. He had been cleaning himself off in a river."

'Have you got him?' Tom asked. I said, "Yes." He said, 'Okay, it's on you.'

"I put my scope's cross hairs on Trang as he stood up and used his shirt to wipe himself off. Then he turned around and was now facing us directly. Calmly, I exhaled half of my second breath; then held it as my fingertip slowly tightened on my trigger."

"Under my breath, I said, 'This is for the little girl, motherfucker.' Then the M14 fired, with the concussion blowing Trang backwards. 'Clean shot,' Tom quietly exclaimed.

"We were then chased out of there by Trang's cohorts firing madly in our direction, just managing to catch our extraction chopper which would wait for us only ten minutes. Tom would later tell me he had his spotter scope on Trang the whole time and then all of a sudden, Trang's head simply disappeared. The little girl survived. One less scumbag in the world." [32]

## Part Four (1966-1976)

While Poe resided in placid Thailand, Tom Fosmire was toiling away in CIA's Saigon Station following his stint as base chief of Military Region 3 in Laos. The CIA contingent in Saigon was quite large, having almost six hundred agents and employees. Until 1972, they were all reporting to Ted Shackley, who had experience running a large field office from his Miami days. Before the peace talks took hold, Shackley had to deal with a CIA operation renowned for its controversy... the Phoenix Program. Bill Lair avoided it but Fosmire may not have.

Started in 1967, the Phoenix Program that sniper Corporal Richards was a part of had its genesis back with Ed Lansdale's Civic Action Program and others initiated during the mid-1950s designed to strengthen President Diem's internal security apparatus. However, during the Diem period, people viewed his forces as more threatening than even the Viet Cong. In fact, until 1959, the Viet Cong actually had a policy of non-violence. In 1960, William Colby instituted the Civilian Irregular Defense Group (CIDG) in which CIA funded Vietnamese Special Forces organized and armed favorable minorities against communist entities. Then the Mountain Scouts Program started, where similar techniques used by the Viet Cong were employed in selected communist villages. The scouts evolved into having hunter-killer teams which not only sought useful intelligence but also took part in kidnapping and assassination. [26, 64]

Later, Provincial Interrogation Centers, called PICS, were built and funded by the CIA cover organization, Pacific Architects and Engineers which also built a similar large facility at Udorn Air Base, Thailand. Eventually, forty-four centers were constructed in South Vietnam where incarcerated suspects were questioned in subpar facilities lacking qualified interrogators and having lax oversight controls. The program degenerated into a means for corrupt Vietnamese to settle old scores or name innocent people simply to obtain bribe money for their release. The Vietnamese, communist and non-communist alike, often viewed torture as an accepted and valid means to obtain information. Bribes were a commonplace practice as well. Atrocious methods were often used as American overseers weren't always around or lacked the resolve to do anything. Phung Hoang came into being on the South Vietnamese side of the program, giving the appearance the CIA were simply involved as advisers. In 1968, the CIA regions were each assigned a military intelligence officer and rifts soon developed between the CIA and the military. General Bruce Palmer outlined the dilemma most succinctly... [26, 64]

> "I don't believe that people in uniform, who are pledged to abide by the Geneva Convention, should be put in the position of having to break those laws of warfare." [26]

Ted Shackley was the man in charge of overseeing the Phoenix Program when he took over Saigon Station in 1968. Aside from Tom Fosmire being reassigned to Vietnam, his fellow comrade from the Tibetan Task Force days, Roger McCarthy, also came aboard. McCarthy was posted to take over Region I, the northernmost being closest to North Vietnam. He had difficulty in cultivating valuable intelligence which Shackley always demanded. The usual thinking was that the 1968 Tet Offensive had now made the Viet Cong a spent force but McCarthy believed otherwise. In his region, the Viet Cong was clearly reconstituting itself by regularly raiding and pillaging refugee centers. As McCarthy related, nobody wanted to hear that since it contradicted prevailing opinions in Washington. McCarthy forwarded his reports to Ted Shackley, nevertheless. [26, 64]

> "Shackley and I had a few heated exchanges about this", McCarthy said. McCarthy also suspected his negative but truth laden reports were never forwarded on to Washington.

A year after Shackley arrived on the job, he began a six-month phase out of Phoenix transferring oversight to CORDS or Civil Operations and Revolutionary Development Support. To him, the cost of poor press image as being an assassination program outweighed the value of any intelligence obtained. Despite the withdrawal, Shackley still maintained watch over the program and some of his agents in the provinces would continue to participate in Phoenix operations. McCarthy said he "raised the bar" to ensure Viet Cong or communist suspects were authenticated first which precluded apprehension of innocent people. Naturally, his numbers then went down as a result, becoming yet another irritant to Shackley who was quantitatively driven. As McCarthy said, "I didn't play the numbers game as most others did." [26, 61]

Another notable aspect of Ted Shackley was the drug and finance business. When he took over as Station Chief in Laos in 1966, Shackley brought in his boys from the agency's Miami office. As already noted, David Morales took over the southern military region of Laos. Tom Clines became Shackley's deputy in Laos and others like Edwin Wilson, Felix Rodriguez, Carl Jenkins and Rafael Quintana followed in as well. When Shackley went to Saigon, the "secret team" followed in tow. Felix Rodriguez arrived later in 1970, after first assisting the Bolivian army in killing Che Guevara. [39, 85]

The story, according to a well-known author, has it that Ted Shackley assisted Vang Pao in establishing a monopoly in the opium business by helping eliminate competitors. In fact, it's even said that Phoenix assassination squads were turned on some of them, alleging they were Vietcong sympathizers. Shackley financed the two planes Vang used to transport opium between Long Cheng and Vientiane and also set up a meeting between Santo Trafficante and Vang Pao in Saigon in 1968. This was to improve sourcing to the US as European authorities were shutting down drug trafficking that had been using using the French Connection. [43]

According to another author, the proceeds from the Vang Pao's drug business funded much of the increased cost of the Phoenix Program and then some. How this was done was learned by Shackley under Paul Helliwell's mentorship in Miami. Helliwell had already relocated his SEA Supply office to the city by the time Shackley took over the Miami field office. [39, 43]

Assisted by Richard Secord and Tom Clines, excess funds were spirited out of Vietnam and deposited in a secret account with the Nugen Hand Bank in Australia. Michael Hand, an ex-Green Beret, had been a CIA operative who was often seen in Laos. The bank became an off-the-books source for funding agency operations. Some authors or sources assert that Shackley's secret team also set up several corporations and subsidiary companies, mostly in Switzerland, which laundered large amounts of Vang Pao's opium money. [39, 85]

Despite a few successes of Phoenix under CORDS, the program was simply considered just "too little too late" and was terminated February 1973, right after the Paris Peace Accords. During its five years of operation, the Phoenix Program was said to have caused the deaths of over twenty-six thousand civilians. The program, despite reasonable first intentions, showed the failing of democracy being morally superior to life under communism. [26]

In February 1972, Shackley was back to headquarters at Langley, taking over the CIA's Western Hemisphere Division with Thomas Polgar now in charge of Saigon Station. Polgar was more relaxed than Shackley and less assuming. He allowed his base chiefs to file their reports directly to Washington and got rid of the unpopular quota system. [27]

As 1975 began, the North Vietnamese were on the move south. By the end of March, Da Nang fell a week after Hue, the old imperial capital. People were frantically streaming to the harbor and airport, with some clinging to the landing gears of planes trying to take off. Fifteen heavily reinforced North Vietnamese divisions then attacked and took Xuon Loc, the last line of defense just twenty-six miles outside Saigon. Other communist forces soon proceeded to encircle Saigon. The Politburo in Hanoi then cabled General Dung, demanding, "Unremitting vigor in the attack all the way to the heart of Saigon." [27, 81]

Tom Polgar tried to put a positive face on developments, saying, "South Vietnam will survive." Tom Fosmire then interrupted his boss, saying he doubted the South Vietnamese military had enough morale to survive. Fosmire's friend and fellow agent, James Parker, also told Polgar that after fighting for decades to unify the country, he doubted the Communists would simply halt right outside Saigon and sue for peace. Parker had intel from a report his source General Hai provided which predicted the final outcome down to the actual date. General

## Part Four (1966-1976)

Hai believed so much in the veracity of his report and the outcome that he committed suicide shortly after providing it to Parker. [27]

CIA Station Chief Polgar was pinning his optimism on recent cables from Henry Kissinger who had been in touch with the Soviets indicating Hanoi possibly willing to form a coalition government in the far south. It was eventually all shown to be a clever ploy by the communists to have South Vietnam lower its guard, facilitating the taking of Saigon. Tom Fosmire later said to Parker after suspecting Polgar was a bit crazy, [27, 81]

> "Crazy or not, the North Vietnamese are going to win this war, flat out, whether that desk warrior likes it or not." [27]

On the last day of April 1975, Saigon fell. Seven thousand people were evacuated under Operation Frequent Wind. Tens of thousands more left on their own volition by air or by boat. By the end of the year, Vientiane would also fall. The theory of toppling dominos which precipitated American involvement to halt the spread of communism in Southeast Asia had stopped. Footholds had been effectively prevented in Thailand, Indonesia and Philippines. As to Saigon, Tom Fosmire would be among the very last Americans to leave.

Within months of signing the Paris Peace Accords, President Nixon and Leonid Brezhnev signed the SALT-I Treaty. The treaty aimed to restrict anti-ballistic missiles, the missiles whose task was to shoot down nuclear warheads. It limited strategic missile defenses to two hundred interceptors each and allowed each side to construct two missile defense sites, one to protect the national capital, the other to protect one Intercontinental Ballistic Missile (ICBM) field. The Soviets had been building ICBMs at an alarming rate and now also anti-ballistic missiles which upset the parity and second-strike capability of the respective countries. It was that parity and deterrence value that kept the arms race in check. [20, 81]

The agreement had some loopholes, however, for instance leaving out heavy bombers and submarine launched nuclear missiles. SALT-II talks began in late 1972, hoping to rectify deficits in SALT-I. SALT-II was signed but it was never ratified by Congress. It's terms were adhered to, however, until such time as START-I, a more comprehensive agreement took over in 1991. Today's American land based intercontinental missiles include the Minuteman III housed in over four hundred launch silos, fourteen nuclear missile submarines with Trident II missiles and from the air, the B2 Stealth bomber and, of course, the ever-reliable B-52 Stratofortress. [81]

# Promise Still Unfulfilled

"You have opened a new chapter in the relations of the American and Chinese people... I am confident that this beginning of our friendship will certainly meet with majority support of our two peoples"

- Chinese Premier Zhou Enlai

Early 1972 had started with great promise. The Nixon-Mao rapprochement seemed to have assured the start of a new world or at least a new chapter as stated above by Zhou Enlai. Zhou had been Mao's right-hand man since the Chinese Civil War, becoming his first premier in 1949. In fact, he was the one who orchestrated the meeting of the leaders in February 1972. He developed the policies China had with other nations including the Soviet Union and the United States, winning the respect of many world leaders, whether communist or not. His actions curtailing the outrages of the Red Guard in later stages of the Cultural Revolution won him the gratitude of legions of Chinese citizens. Zhou was essentially the good cop counterpart to Mao's bad cop. [1, 20, 81]

Shortly after the Mao meeting with Nixon, it was discovered that Zhou had cancer of the bladder. Under an incredulous edict at the time, the doctors had to report first to Mao who alone would decide on medical decisions "in the interest of national security." Mao specifically ordered the doctors to:

"Keep it secret. Do not tell Zhou or his wife. No examination and no surgery." [1]

Mao's reasoning was that Zhou was already seventy-four years and had heart problems so surgery would be useless. This ignored the fact that Mao had worse medical problems and was, in fact, four years older. Mao, of course, had his own medical team always ready should anything happen to him. Zhou firmly believed in communism but carefully departed from Mao's increasingly fanatical ways. He always slavishly deferred to his boss holding him in highest regard whenever they appeared together. But Mao was wary of the power Zhou had, oddly the same power he himself bestowed on Zhou over the army, the Party and Chinese government. Most importantly, Mao did not want Zhou to outlive him. [1]

So Mao had the man, that he withheld a medical diagnosis from, required to issue a detailed self-denunciation of his past mistakes in front of three hundred party officials.

It was Mao again revisiting his sadistic side. For Zhou, it was a humiliating exercise but he had no choice to show that he presented no threat to Mao. He did what he was told and by 1973, Zhou's urine had blood in it. Still Mao declined any medical treatment even though Zhou had become aware of his condition. Zhou humbly requested that he be allowed the surgery. Mao finally granted the request on condition that:

> "The surgery had to be done in two stages. The first just being an exploratory examination and if any tumor is found, it would be left to the second surgery to remove it." [1]

When they went in, the surgeons risked Mao's wrath by removing the growth anyway, figuring they wouldn't be given another opportunity. Mao, realizing the deed had already been done, oddly remarked that it was a good decision that the doctors combined the two stages into one. [1]

Mao was informed that Nixon had signed the SALT-I treaty with Brezhnev in May 1972, just three months after his own meeting with Nixon. He had hoped his own meeting would have given a boost to his faltering Superpower Program, by holding out the possibility of a military alliance with the US. But the SALT treaty

# Part Four (1966-1976)

confirmed for Mao that there really were only two major powers in the world: the US and the Soviet Union. [1, 81]

To Mao, his historic meeting in Beijing was more about China benefiting from transference of American military technology than it was about building mutual understanding and friendship between the two peoples. Watergate and Nixon's resignation was made to blame, which the Chairman just couldn't understand what all the fuss was about. [1]

> "Do leaders not have the right to rule?" Mao was known
> to have asked Thailand's prime minister. [1]

Zhou's cancer returned and Mao began blaming his Premier as much as he did the Watergate proceedings for China's technology malaise. In May 1974, Zhou's condition became worse, and he soon required weekly blood transfusions. Mao initially ruled out any more surgeries but he later relented. Two years after his diagnosis, any full operation was now considered too late and Zhou Enlai died over a year later. In January 1976, he was the first to go but Mao himself also had his own serious medical issues. News of Zhou's death resulted in an outpouring of grief throughout China, with a million people known to have lined the streets of Beijing. Crowds swarmed Tianamen Square, bringing wreaths and flowers but Mao himself refused to attend, let alone publicly say any words. Riots broke out as police violently tried to disperse the crowds. The crowds were not just mourning Zhou Enlai. They were expressing their contempt for Mao's policies under which they'd been living for so many years. Policies which originally had an auspicious beginning. [1]

Leading up to the founding of the People's Republic of China in October 1949, Mao had been in extensive discussions with other parties in developing a Common Program. The program included the democratic notions of free search, assembly and publication. The bourgeoisie class would, of course, be eliminated in the near future with their land going to the peasants. There seemed to be general agreement amongst all the parties as to the agreed principles of the

Common Program. By the following summer, with Mao Tse-Tung now fully entrenched at the top, things took a dramatic and troubling turn.

> "All the intellectuals got was to be 'reformed', while the workers were forbidden to strike and forbidden to set up any independent labor unions. Property owners 'voluntarily' donated all their assets, while the entire Chinese people got a 'republic' in which they weren't even allowed to vote.
>
> "Mao's legacy, at the very least, includes the silencing of public opinion, an unelected regime, collusion between the three governmental powers, and the mass manufacture of miscarriages of justice.
>
> "Most important among these is undoubtedly the absolute power of the leadership, because whoever holds this, holds in their hand the power of hundreds of millions of workers. Such was the so-called mighty victory of the democratic revolution, the basis of the myth of Mao Tse-Tung." [87]
>
> - Bao Tong, aide to ousted Premier Zhao Ziyang

Just after midnight on September 9, 1976, Mao Tse-Tung died without having appointed a successor or even leaving a will. His legacy measured in human lives and suffering was devastating. According to the 1994 Washington Post article, "How Many Died?" by Valerie Strauss and Daniel Southerl,

> "One government document that has been internally circulated and seen by a former Communist Party official now at Princeton University says that 80 million died unnatural deaths... most of them in the famine following the Great Leap Forward. This figure comes from the Tigaisuo, or the System Reform Institute, which was led by Zhao Ziyang, the deposed Communist Party

chief, in the 1980s to study how to reform Chinese society" [86]

The myth of Mao is still strongly maintained today, almost fifty years after his death.

# Epilogue

The Central Intelligence Agency had grown and struggled since its founding in 1947 charting a path through the Cold War, often in times of great discord, controversy and intrigue. The year 1975 was called the "Year of Intelligence" for good reason as it was then that the Senate Select Committee to Study Government Operations or commonly referred to as the Church Committee took form. The committee investigated abuses by the FBI, the NSA, the IRS and importantly also the CIA. It's where MK ULTRA was brought to light as well as "Family Jewels" detailing assassination attempts including on Fidel Castro's life as well as numerous other violations of the CIA's original charter. [81]

CIA Director William Colby would call disclosed reports, "skeletons in the CIA's closet." Most of the documents were finally released by June 2007, after three decades of secrecy. The House counterpart to the Church committee was the Pike Committee formed the same year with a major difference between the committees, being that Pike found the CIA didn't act alone. They were under direction of the President and, to a certain degree, his Secretary of State. The Third option, between using diplomacy or going to war, which Eisenhower so cherished, had, by the 1970s, the markings of being an "imperial presidency" with its unchecked power. As Chairman Otis Pike said: [81]

> "The major things which are done are not done unilaterally by the CIA without approval from higher up the line. The CIA never did anything the White House did not want. In fact, sometimes they didn't want to do the things that they did." [81]

## Epilogue

Both the Church and Pike committees were supplemented by the President's Commission on CIA Activities within the United States. It was also known as the Rockefeller Commission, which brought to light details of Project MK Ultra and Sidney Gottleib's involvement in heading the LSD/Mind Control program. Richard Cheney, acting deputy White House Chief of Staff is known to have said the Rockefeller Commission was actually set up to preclude congressional attempts to further infringe on the executive branch. [81]

An executive branch, with unrestricted control over a clandestine organization such as the CIA, using unvouchered accounts and dubious funding sources, is a dangerous precedent. The distinction between the US government and Mao's China become blurred with the only saving grace being we have term limits, rule of law and press freedom which, in due course, are endangered to become diluted as well. Having a clandestine organization in a free and open democratic society presents a tough balancing act. But balance they must since at the end of the day, we do need an effective and responsible CIA to protect our country and our way of life.

Long Cheng today can now be visited and one can see the house where Vang Pao lived, tour Skyline Ridge and explore other notable features. Camp Hale has been open for years, however, the original structures are long gone except for a few concrete emplacements. Both areas are still dealing with removal of old ordnance which can be occasionally found. The legacies of war, unlike the participating actors, still choose to linger on.

Unlike his fellow agents, Vint Lawrence didn't spend twenty or thirty years with the CIA. After three years in Laos, he had enough after frequently seeing the dark side of humanity. Lawrence's personal character was not lost on Vang Pao nor the Hmong people themselves. He was said to have been given one of the biggest "baci" or going away ceremonies. Heading back back to the US for a brief stint as an aide to Director Colby, he then decided to get out for good. Wars, conflicts and the clandestine service was simply not his calling. Vint Lawrence went on to make his mark in life as a renowned caricature artist for the

Washington Post and New Republic magazine. He passed away in 2016 at age 76.

Tony Poe retired from the CIA in 1975 when he was awarded his second Intelligence Star, equivalent to the military's Silver Star. He stayed in Thailand with his family until 1992 when he returned to the US and was active with the Hmong community in Northern California. Occasionally, he would return to Thailand to assist Hmong still trying to escape into Thailand, while angering the authorities. Before he died in 2003, he often reminisced about the old days in Laos, freely admitting with a measure of pride, his brutal acts to journalists. Poe insisted that his motive was to defeat communism, yet the acts and heavy drinking didn't start until he went to Laos. When discussing his time at Camp Hale, Tony Poe ranked the tall, fierce Khampas of Tibet as the best fighters he had ever trained. Despite much barbarism attributed to Poe, the agency felt Tony Poe in many ways set the template for future CIA paramilitary training and procedures.

Tom Fosmire, after the fall of Saigon in 1975, went on to conduct paramilitary training in El Salvador and Honduras. He passed away in 2007. The CIA, on its Trailblazers page, recognized his superior operational and training skills, including instruction of newer agents. They particularly noted Fosmire leading his crew back to safety after being shot down four days previously behind enemy lines during the Vietnam War. Tom Fosmire was twice awarded the CIA's prestigious Intelligence Medal of Merit.

Bill Lair, somewhat disappointed he wasn't promoted to Station Chief, stayed on in Thailand with his Thai wife. He had invested much of his life to the betterment of Southeast Asia and carried the Thai rank of colonel. The CIA preferred its agents not "go native" as Lair had done but rather, like Ted Shackley, to remain cold and detached when going about the agency's business. Before being transferred back to the US, he was given a private audience with H.M. King Bhumibol, of Thailand in recognition of his contribution to Thailand's security. Bill Lair was active in the Hmong American community when he returned to the states and passed away 2014 at age 90. Today, the Lao and

## Epilogue

Hmong contributions in the Secret War are commemorated with a memorial plaque at Arlington National Cemetery.

Roger McCarthy, after Vietnam, eventually left the agency, writing the successful, "Tears of the Lotus" in 1997 about CIA involvement in the Tibetan resistance. He passed away ten years following its publication. A Tibetan commemoration ceremony was held and plaque installed in September 2010 at Camp Hale, attended by many guests including several agents from the period. McCarthy was aptly represented by his son, Kevin, who spoke fondly of his father's involvement as head of the Tibetan Task Force. On October 13, 2022, President Biden formally designated Camp Hale and surrounding eighty-four square mile area, the Camp Hale-Continental Divide National Monument.

One recent brisk morning, a young Tibetan American ventured up to Camp Hale and proceeded to lay several prayer scarves onto the memorial plaque, remembering Tibetan training there and the sacrifice freedom fighters made over sixty years ago. After carefully laying the scarves, the man began his chant-like prayers. It was a beautiful day in late spring Colorado with much of the valley floor already bursting in a profusion of colorful mountain wildflowers. The floral mosaic comes back every year more vibrant and pervasive than before, despite the forest fires, harsh winters and other calamities. Much like the human spirit during periods of war, repression and tyranny, there remains a powerful will to survive. They always find some way to regenerate, to thrive and carry on.

# Afterword

In 1946, Winston Churchill gave his famous Iron Curtain speech at Westminster College in Missouri...

> "Neither the sure prevention of war, nor the continuous rise of world organization will be gained without what I have called the fraternal association of the English-speaking peoples. This means a special relationship between the British Commonwealth and Empire and the United States... the continuance of the intimate relationship between our military advisers, leading to common study of potential dangers..."

It was a relationship born of common ideals, joint interest and shared hardships fighting on the same side in two world wars. Like siblings, there was occasionally discord and disagreement but, in the end, the allies hung together particularly when there was a new villain on the block to deal with. By 1946, communism was rapidly spreading: being relentlessly pushed and prodded by Stalin. The bond strengthened with US/UK collaboration on German code breaking at Bletchley Park in 1941, and continued into 1943 with the BRUSA Agreement. By 1960, the pact to share and collaborate on intelligence gathering also included Canada, Australia and New Zealand and later came to be referred to as Five Eyes or ECHELON. The Five Eyes arrangement, considered one of world's most comprehensive spying alliances, is very much in operation today and now includes as third-party partners, Norway, Germany, Japan and others as well. In

# Afterword

military parlance, Five Eyes is akin to a force multiplier greatly expanding the scope of American espionage capability on a worldwide basis.

A counterpart to the CIA is the National Security Agency (NSA) which was established in late 1952. It was an outgrowth of the Armed Forces Security Agency initially under the Joint Chiefs of Staff but came to its own on that date, albeit still under Department of Defense command. Essentially, the CIA deals with human intelligence, whereas the NSA handles electronic intelligence, but they often work together on matters of mutual interest. When the PBJointly Project involving tapping Soviet communication lines in Berlin occurred in 1954, Jim Harvey of the CIA was put in charge, even though it was primarily a signals intercept. It was the NSA that provided evidence of the North Vietnamese attack in the USS Maddox leading to the Gulf of Tonkin incident and deepening America's involvement in the Vietnam War. The British counterpart to the NSA is the Government Communications Headquarters (GCHQ).

The world has changed since the mid-1970s, following the Vietnamese War and congressional hearings into the CIA, FBI and NSA. But, in some respects, it hasn't really changed much at all. Terrorism raised its ugly head in the following decades, necessitating a continuing need for human intelligence and para-military operations as earlier practiced by Tony Poe and his cohorts in Laos. However, the need for signals intelligence never abated; if anything, it greatly increased. Cold War adversaries never went away, Communist China is still here, the Soviet Union changed its name but not its ways and, of course, we still have the ever-belligerent North Korea to contend with.

As communications technology advanced, so did electronic espionage, the means to eavesdrop on what adversaries were doing or planning to do. Advance notice gave us extra warning and reaction time and intelligence provided insight into enemy's capabilities and needed countermeasures. Measures emphasizing the role espionage began in earnest, shortly after World War II. The accumulated rubble from allied bombing of Berlin became the city's highest point called Teufelsberg, or Devils Peak, which was topped with listening radars pointed towards Moscow. It was also known as Field Station Berlin, where up to 1,500 military personnel worked in three shifts around the clock until operations finally ceased in 1989. At the same time Berlin Station started, another listening post was established at Bad Aibling to the south in Bavaria. That Cold War radar site was turned over to the Germans in 2004, which continued to share their intercepted data with the NSA. Menwith Hill in England is yet another location which performs similar tasks, including intelligence sharing with the NSA.

Much of communication today, including the burgeoning internet, travels around the world by undersea fiber optic cables. Working with the CIA and US Navy, NSA taps into sections of these cables, which are no larger in diameter than a garden hose. The lines lie on the ocean floor but are covered up as they approach the shoreline. In some instances, NSA has arranged infiltration with a host country where the lines make landfall. There are presently about 500 lines throughout the world with a line typically lasting 25 years before replacement is needed. One line, named the Polar Express, skirts across on the northern edge of Russia, Other lines run from Taiwan to Quemoy Island and also Matsu, providing early warning in case of a Chinese attack. Unsurprisingly, there are no undersea cables connected to or from North Korea.

Satellites are already the next frontier of communications with a proliferation of them orbiting the earth today, transmitting communications, electronic guidance for aircraft and missiles and taking reconnaissance photos of the earth below. Of course, NSA uses their own to spy on Five Eyes' adversaries and its satellites. The first NSA satellite was launched into low orbit in 1960, originally under the guise of being for scientific study. Syncomm-II was put up in 1963 into geosynchronous orbit, which tracks the earth's rotation, thereby always being over the same spot on earth. The CIA also remained deeply involved and by 1966, Project Rainfall was initiated as a ground radar station in central Australia near Alice Springs. The Pine Gap site controls a configuration of three geosynchronous Orion satellites covering much of the globe, focusing on the Asian continent, including nations of greatest concern. They tap in on communications during uplinks and downlinks of targeted satellites and also instrumentation data providing telemetry information for enemy missiles. Other

# Afterword

information provided includes infrared imaging possibly indicating blasts from missile launches.

In December 2022, there was an unveiling of America's new B-21 stealth high-altitude, long-range bomber by Northrop Grumman. Aside from being stealthier, smaller and able to carry both conventional and nuclear bombs, this 6th generation bomber is expected to replace the B-2 and B-1B bombers. It won't replace the perennial favorite B-52 which, following a number of upgrades, will continue to be around for years to come. Plans call for the first test flights of the B-21 to be held next year and production ramped up to supply the Air Force, but not until 2027. So, why the public unveiling now?

It's sending a message. Aside from the US, there are only two other countries in the world having a strategic bomber force: China and Russia. According to a recent Pentagon report, the Chinese has doubled its nuclear warheads and is on track to produce 1,500 nuclear weapons by 2035... much sooner than originally anticipated. The hope is that the early unveiling will act as a deterrent to the Chinese nuclear threat and recent Russian aggression. Most likely, it will not. In a world replete with spying, arms proliferation and conflict, some things never seem to change.

# Photographs

Tony Poe

Bill Lair

Tom Fosmire

Roger McCarthy

Vint Lawrence

All photographs have permissions given or are public domain

All photographs have permissions given or are public domain

Marpi Point, Saipan

CIA Facility, Camp Hale
Colorado

Long Cheng, Laos

# List of Maps

# References

1.  Chang, Jung and Holliday, Jon. Mao- The Unknown Story (2006)

2.  Weiner, Tim. Legacy of Ashes- The History of the CIA (2007)

3.  Lui, Xiaojuan. To the End of Revolution (2020)

4.  Kinzer, Stephen. The Brothers- John Foster Dulles, Allen Dulles & Their Secret War (2014)

5.  Holobar, Frank. Raiders of the China Coast (1999)

6.  Downey, John T. Lost in the Cold War- The Story of Jack Downey (2022)

7.  Anderson, Scott. The Quiet Americans (2020)

8.  Tanner, Harold M. Where Chiang Kai-shek Lost China (2015)

9.  Bath, David W. Assured Destruction- Building the Ballistic Missile Culture in the US Air Force (2020)

10. Hayton, Bill. The Invention of China (2020)

11. Endo, Homare. Japanese Girl at the Siege of Changchun (2012)

12. Drury, Bob and Clavin, Tom. The Last Stand of Fox Company (2009)

13. Cleaver, Thomas Mckelvey. The Frozen Chosen (2016)

14. Gaddis, John Lewis. The Cold War- A New History (2005)

15. Halberstam, David. The Coldest Winter- America and the Korean War (2007)

16. Bevins, Vincent. The Jakarta Method (2020)

# References

17. Hancock, Larry. Shadow Warfare- The History of America's Undeclared War (2014)

18. Gauthier, Brandon. Before Evil- Young Lenin, Stalin & Mao (2022)

19. Jeans, Roger B. The CIA and Third Force Movements in China During the Early Cold War (2018)

20. Kissinger, Henry. Henry Kissinger on China (2011)

21. Saich, Tony. From Rebel to Ruler- 100 Years of the Chinese Communist Party (2021)

22. Shackley, Ted. Spymaster- My Life in the CIA (2005)

23. Kurlantzick, Joshua. A Great Place to Have a War- America in Laos (2016)

24. Schofield, Steven. The Secret War in Laos- Green Berets, CIA and the Hmong (2019)

25. Taubman, William. Khruschev- The Man and His Era (2004)

26. Valentine, Douglas. The Phoenix Program (1990)

27. Clarke, Thurston. Honorable Exit (2019)

28. Ross, Colin A M.D. The CIA Doctors (2006)

29. Starfire. MK ULTRA Dark Labs 1959-1975 (2019)

30. Henderson, Bruce. Hero Found- The Greatest Pow Escape of the Vietnam War (2010)

31. Davis, Peter E. B-52 Stratofortress vs SA-2 Guideline SAM (2018)

32. Dohrman, Samual. Operation Phoenix in Vietnam (2021)

33. Parker, James E. Battle for Skyline Ridge (2019)

34. Conboy, Kenneth and Morrison, James. The CIA's Secret War in Laos (2002)

35. Rottman, Gordon L. North Vietnamese Army Soldier 1958-1975 (2012)

36. McCoy, Alfred. The Politics of Heroin (2003)

37. National Museum of the USAF. Stories of Sacrifice and Dedication- CAT, Air America and the CIA (2011)

38. Warner, Roger. Shooting at the Moon (1996)

39. Corn, David. Blond Ghost- Ted Shackley and the CIA's Crusades (1994)

40. Conboy, Kenneth and Morrison, James. Feet to the Fire- CIA Operations in Indonesia (1999)

41. Knaus, John Kenneth. Orphans of the Cold War (1999)

42. Graebner, Norman. The National Security- Its Theory and Practice (1986)

43. Trento, Joseph J. Prelude to Terror- Legacy of America's Private Intelligence Network (2005)

44. Dunham, Mike. Buddha's Warriors- Story of CIA Backed Tibetan Freedom Fighters (2004)

45. Wetmore, Karen. Surviving Evil- CIA Mind Control Experiments in Vermont (2014)

46. Cha, Ya Pa. An Introduction to Hmong Culture (2010)

47. Curry, Cecil B. Victory at Any Cost- The Genius of General Vo Nguyen Giap (1997)

48. Goliszek Andrew. In the Name of Science (2003)

49. Strangio, Sebastian. In the Dragon's Shadow- Southeast Asia in the Chinese Century (2020)

50. Thomas, Evan. The Very Best Men- The Daring Early Years of the CIA (2006)

51. Burton, M.H. Quiet Spy, Secret War- Life and Times of James William Lair (2019)

52. Ahern, Thomas L. Jr. Undercover Armies: CIA and Surrogate Warfare in Laos. (2006)

53. Proietti , Matt. At All Costs- The True Story of Vietnam War Hero CMSgt Dick Etchberger (2006)

54. Burchett, Wilfred G. Mekong Upstream: A Visit to Laos and Cambodia. (1959)

55. Interview with Vint Lawrence, by Paul Hillmer (2006)

56. The Flame that Flickered and Died, by Col. Michael E. Haas (1996)

# References

57. Air America in Thailand, by Dr. Joe E. Leeker (2015)

58. The Perils of Chrome Dome, by Rebecca Grant (2011)

59. What is the Difference Between a Hydrogen Bomb and an Atomic Bomb, by Melissa Chan (unk)

60. War From Above the Clouds- B52 Operations in Indochina, William P. Head (2002)

61. The Ho Chi Minh Trail, by John T. Cornell (2005)

62. Secret Alliance: CIA and Indian Intelligence in Tibet, by GreatGameIndia (2020)

63. War Gaming Methodology, by M.G. Weiner (1960)

64. The Phoenix Program and Contemporary Counterinsurgency, by William Rosenau and Austin Long (2009)

65. Operation Paper- The United States and Drugs in Thailand and Burma, by Peter Dale Scott (2010)

66. Psychological Operations- A Force Multiplier, by Joseph D. Celeski (2019)

67. China and Laos- 1945-1979, by Frederic C. Benson (2019)

68. CIA Intelligence Memorandum- Communist Aid to North Vietnam, by Director Economic Research (1968)

69. On Wargaming- How War Games Have Shaped History & How They May Shape the Future, by Matthew B. Caffrey, Jr. (2019)

70. Opium Poppy Cultivation and Heroin Processing in Southeast Asia, by DEA (1992)

71. JACK Operations & Activities Korea 1951-1953 by Charles H. Briscoe (unk)

72. CIA Memo to the President - Threat of Chinese Invasion of Korea, Formosa & Indochina, by Director Walter B. Smith (Oct 1950)

73. Taiwan's Offshore Islands- Pathway or Barrier?, by Brice A. Elleman (2019)

74. The Joint Chiefs of Staff and National Policy 1945-1950, 1950-1952, 1953-1954, 1957-1960, 1961-1964, 1965-1968, and 1969-1972

75. Post-War Mountain Training, by LtCol. Erwin G. Nilsson (1955)

76. Memo- Discussion With the President on Tibet, by Gordon Gray (1960)

77. The Question of Tibet and Rule of Law, by International Commission of Jurists (1959)

78. The Chinese People's Liberation Army in the 1960s, by Randall Vincent Lewis (1970)

79. Logistical Problems of the Tibetan Campaign, by Central Intelligence Agency (1959) - [redacted]

80. Building Better Games for a National Security Policy Analysis, by Elizabeth M. Bartels (2020)

81. Wikipedia

82. Personal Interviews with Charley Troxel, Mercy Trujillo, David Rivera, Robert Tresize and Ella Burnett, by co-author Deb Turnbull Devries (2021, 2022)

83. The Fall of Lima Site 85, by Capt. Edward Vallentiny, USAF` (1968)

84. Pentagon Papers, by National Archives-attached Pdfs (renewed 2019)

85. Ted Shackley, by John Simpkin/Spartacus-Educational (2022)

86. How Many Died? by Valerie Strauss/Washington Post (1994)

87. The Myths of Mao Zedong Still Haunts China, by Bao Tong/Radio Free Asia (2013)

88. The CIA's Secret Funding and the Constitution, The Yale Law Journal. (1975)

89. How Ping Ping Diplomacy Thawed the Cold War, by Evan Andrews. (2016)

90. Personal Interview with "Tony", Chamorro schoolteacher who lived on Saipan and Guam, by author Randall Howlett (2022)

91. Titan I Missile System by The Military Standard (2010)

92. Spartacus

## References

93.  Mitchell, Greg The Tunnels  (2016)

94.  Koehler, John, O.  Stasi- The Untold Story of the East German Police (1999)

95.  Funder, Anna Stasiland- Stories from Behind the Berlin Wall 2003)

96.  MacGreger, Iain Checkpoint Charlie- The Cold War, the Berlin Wall and the Most Dangerous Place on Earth (2019)

97.  Stanford, David Spies Beneath Berlin (2002)

98.  Tusa, John and Ann The Berlin Airlift- The Cold War Mission to Save a City (2019)

99.  Halvorsen, Gail The Candy Bomber- Untold Stories of the Berlin Airlift (2017)

100. Rob1blackops History of US High-Altitude SIGINT System (2017) Satelliteobservation.nett

101. Wikipedia Five Eyes & Echelon (present day)

102. Wikipedia Berlin Field Station (Teufelsberg), Germany

103. Wikipedia Bad Aibling Station, Germany

104. Wikipedia Menwith Hill Station, United Kingdom

105. Wikipedia Pine Gap Station, Australia

106. Ward, Mark, BBC Q & A: What you need to know about Echelon (2001)

107. Telegeography Worldwide Submarine Cable Map (2022)

108. Rob1blackops Signal Intelligence 101: SIGINT Targets (2017) Satelliteobservation.nett

109. Interview with Tony Poe by Richard Ehrlich (2002)

110. Faderman & Xiong I Begin My Life All Over: The Hmong and Immigrant Experience  (1998)

# The Authors

## Randall Howlett

Randall is a 69-year-old retired and divorced American who has been living in Bangkok for the last ten years enjoying the life as an expat. Prior to that, he worked in middle management for a major insurance company for about 20 years after doing a stint as a Captain in the US Marine Corps for six years. He has a BA in Psychology from Mesa State College, an MA in Business Administration from National University in San Diego and an MBA in Finance/ Real Estate from the University of Denver. Randall had taken up writing books several years ago, focusing mostly on historical nonfiction.

## Deb Turnbull Devries

Deb is a native of the Eagle County, Colorado area where much of this story takes place. She is a retired teacher and a grandmother presently living in Wisconsin. She has a BS in Business Education from Northern Michigan University, an MA in Educational Administration from the same institution and an MA from Central Michigan in Library Science. Deb worked as a high school business teacher and also adjunct university professor for a number of years earning her many teaching awards in Michigan. Her specialty today is conducting deep research.

Both Randall Howlett and Deb Turnbull Devries graduated from the same class of 1971at Battle Mountain High School, located in Colorado's high country.

Made in the USA
Columbia, SC
04 August 2023

21214270R00130